D0886256

The Path of
Brotherhood

CLIMB THE HIGHEST MOUNTAIN SERIES

The Path of Brotherhood

Mark L. Prophet · Elizabeth Clare Prophet

The Everlasting Gospel

SUMMIT UNIVERSITY PRESS

Corwin Springs, Montana

THE PATH OF BROTHERHOOD
by Mark L. Prophet and Elizabeth Clare Prophet
Copyright © 2003 by Summit University Press
All rights reserved

No part of this book may be reproduced; translated; electronically
stored, posted or transmitted; or used in any format or medium
whatsoever without written permission, except by a reviewer who
may quote brief passages in a review. For information, please contact
Summit University Press, PO Box 5000, Corwin Springs, MT 59030-5000.
Tel: 1-800-245-5445 or 406-848-9500.
Web site: www.summituniversitypress.com
E-mail: info@summituniversitypress.com

Library of Congress Catalog Card Number: 2002114153
ISBN: 0-922729-82-4

SUMMIT UNIVERSITY ॐ PRESS
Climb the Highest Mountain, Summit University Press,
Keepers of the Flame, *Pearls of Wisdom*, Teachings of the Ascended Masters,
Science of the Spoken Word and ॐ are registered trademarks.
All rights to their use are reserved.

Layout and design: Lynn Wilbert

Printed in the United States of America

Cover: "Wanderer from the Resplendent City," a painting by Nicholas
Roerich. Nicholas Roerich Museum, New York, N.Y. Used by permission.

Note: Because gender-neutral language can be cumbersome and at times
confusing, we have often used he and him to refer to God or the individual.
These terms are for readability only and are not intended to exclude
women or the feminine aspect of the Godhead. Likewise, our use of
God or Spirit does not exclude other expressions for the Divine.

08   07   06   05   04   03   6   5   4   3   2   1

To all who look for salvation in this age,
to all who know that the hour is come
when the true worshipers shall worship
the Father-Mother God in Spirit and in Truth,
to all who would climb the highest mountain,
we dedicate this volume as the next step.

Note to the Reader

The *Climb the Highest Mountain* series has been outlined in thirty-three chapters by the Ascended Master El Morya. This book contains chapter 14, "Brotherhood."

Contents

Section IV · "I and My Mother Are One" The Mother Flame   63

Section V · World Communism: Counterfeit of the Golden-Age Culture   93

Section VI · The Twelve Tribes of Israel   121

Section VIII • Christ, the Immaculate Concept "I Greet Thee, Lord"   175

Figures

Introduction

THE PURPOSE OF THIS BOOK IS TO show the disciple on the path of Christhood how to transfer the lessons of previous volumes to larger dimensions of consciousness, a larger circle of self-awareness that includes the family, the community, the city, the state, the nation, the hemisphere and the entire earth.

In the second volume in this series, *The Path of Self-Transformation,* we spoke of the Garden of Eden and the story of Adam and Eve. The Garden of Eden is symbolical of the great sphere of consciousness into which God placed the souls of man and woman to work out their salvation. Here they would be taught the seven steps to precipitation that the Elohim had evoked as the answer to the call of the Creator for the creation to come forth. Here they would be taught the mastery of the seven rays of the Christ consciousness in the seven centers of God-awareness, and the path of initiation in the five secret rays. Here they would learn the integration of the energies of East and West through the eighth ray of integration and the Eightfold Path of the Buddha.

Lord Maitreya was the great initiator who was referred to as the LORD God who planted the garden of the Christ consciousness eastward in Eden and walked and talked with man and woman, instructing them in the use of the sacred fire, the energies of God sealed in electrodes—the Tree of Life, which held the consciousness of God, the tree of knowledge of good and evil, which held the consciousness of Christ, and twelve trees "pleasant to the sight, and good for food"[1] holding the soul consciousness.

The story of the coming of Maitreya, the Initiator, to earth's evolutions is told in the first seven chapters of the Book of Genesis. We are concerned with this history because it provides us with a key for the return to the Path where we find once again the true teacher and the true teaching. We are concerned to understand how and why our human ancestors left the Path and where and when we may return to that path.

After his expulsion from Eden, mankind faced the testings of his soul in the relative good and evil whose knowledge he had gained by his original disobedience. His failure to meet these tests is recorded in the Bible, and the LORD's response was the alchemy of the Flood, by which the earth was purified again by the water element.

Whereas the path of initiation involves obedience to the Guru representing the Christ Self, the knower of the absolute Reality of the karma of God, the testing outside of the path of initiation is provided for those among mankind who would begin their way back to the path of redemption by responding to the laws of man. His testing, then, would be according to his knowledge of good and evil and not according to his innocence of that knowledge that he retained while he was yet centered in the true Existence, the true knowledge and the true bliss of the One.

This is why obedience to the Guru supersedes obedience to the right and wrong mandates of a man-made ethic. Obedience to the Guru prepares the chela for the return to the original relationship man and woman had with the Lord—the Christ, the Initiator Maitreya. When man and woman demonstrate a new willingness to be obedient to God's laws and to the teachers of those laws, there comes the moment when they are reinstated in the Edenic consciousness that they knew before they ate of the fruit of the tree of the knowledge of good and evil. Freed by their own free will from the limitations of human goodness and human badness, they may once again pursue in obedience the living flame of the only one that is Good—God.

We have seen the karma that man has created by making himself a law unto himself, and in this volume we will explore the methods and the means whereby man and woman can return to the state of grace. Reembodiment provides man and woman the opportunity to retrace every step they have taken outside of the Garden of Eden, step by step, reaping in full measure the past sowings of good and evil in time and space.

Reembodiment was originally provided by God as the opportunity for the soul to fulfill thirty-three steps on the path of initiation. Now man and woman have created their own path of initiation, and their own karma has become the initiator, the interpreter and the integrator of the laws of mortality and immortality. Now the period of reembodiment—greatly extended since the Fall—is the means whereby man and woman return to life in Eden where the path of initiation begins.

In this book we will consider how the foundations of culture, human institutions of government, commerce, religion and education show the ritual of the seven rays or their perversions in the spiritual/material civilizations of mankind. Their transforming effect on the human soul shows their alchemical attributes to bring the individual under the dominion of the Real Self or the dominance of the synthetic self. The evolution of the concept of the individual, his importance as the link in Hierarchy, and a stone in the pyramid of civilization until he becomes the chief cornerstone in the temple—the Christ, the keystone of the age—tells us the uses and misuses of spiritual/material freedom.

The element of transmutation, the supreme test of the collective karma of the group mandala of the cities and the nations to transmute the material city of man into the spiritual City of God—from the tents of the Israelites to the New Jerusalem, the City Foursquare—the culmination of the seventh ray is seen in the total transformation of society from individual self-mastery to self-mastery in the interaction of the entire Body of God. This law of interaction is the figure eight of karma—the law of integration.

This book is a handbook dedicated by the Mother to her children. It is the World Mother who takes her children by the hand and introduces them to the path of initiation and to the Great Initiator, Lord Maitreya. It is Maitreya who gives the teaching, who introduces each disciple to the Master who will personify to him the Christed One serving on one of the seven rays, who will tutor his soul and bring him to the feet of his own Christ Self. It is to Lord Maitreya who has fused the consciousness of Christ and Buddha and the paths of East and West that we dedicate this book.

Mark L. Prophet

Elizabeth Clare Prophet

MARK L. PROPHET AND ELIZABETH CLARE PROPHET
Messengers for the Great White Brotherhood

Brotherhood

Am I my brother's keeper?

GENESIS

Section I

"I and My Father Are One"

"I and My Father Are One"

"**B**ROTHERHOOD IS MANIFEST IN THE twining of human energies around the heart of God, fired into shining bands of golden understanding and forged by illumination's golden flame. Brotherhood: How like a mirage you have seemed to men!" —EL MORYA

The Desire to Create after the Divine Similitude

The desire of Spirit to create form has yielded the product of individual manifestation. As all came forth from God and all are made in the similitude of God, the concept of brotherhood is the simple acknowledgment that every individual manifestation of life ought to be loved for its intrinsic divine similitude.

In chapter 1 of *Climb the Highest Mountain: The Path of the Higher Self*, we discussed how the synthetic man was formed within man's consciousness, providing a mask of personality that concealed rather than revealed the internal Divine Image. This mask so concealed man's true identity that it also warped his sense of brotherhood. For he could not see the Real Image in himself or in others, and it is only in this image that the concept of brotherhood can be discerned.

The sign of the coming of Maitreya is the sign of brotherhood. Brotherhood is the integration, the interrelation and the cooperation of sons and daughters of God—not necessarily in outer manifestation but in the oneness of the fires of the heart.

Lord Lanto, a member of the spiritual Hierarchy, says: "There are many things undreamed of by humanity that even your science-fiction writers could not in their imagination possibly realize of the reality of Universal Law, which is made known to the Ascended Beings in cosmic councils and schools of holy wisdom. We are eager to impart this knowledge to mankind for his edification and upliftment that the world no longer careen upon her mad course of destruction wherein the little children become the victims of an educational system calculated to bring men into socialistic dimensions.

"We are concerned that men shall understand that the brotherhood of man is a spiritual manifestation whereby the soul can take delight in obtaining holy wisdom. Men can live together in peace and beauty under divine direction with an ultimate restoration of the priest-kings into the world of form as the Ascended Masters step through the veil and manifest the kingdom of heaven before the gaze of humanity. So, rather than have such a small number as five or ten ascensions per year, we may bring millions to that great release of cosmic endeavor whereby they are free at last to graduate from the schools of this world, to matriculate into cosmic dimensions and to feel the enfolding of the Spirit for themselves as the nurturing of humanity by the Brothers of Light from higher dimensions.

"We urge upon you, then, a realization of your great future in the cosmic realm as mankind begins to cast off and overthrow those unfortunate manifestations that are devilish and evil upon the planetary body and replace them, one and all, by those Ascended Master concepts and ideals that are the fruit of the Spirit in righteousness, peace and joy manifest before God upon the altar of everlasting life."[1]

The Law of Affinities

"Birds of a feather flock together" is a statement of the law of affinities (or the law of attraction). It simply means that people are drawn or magnetized to those who think with them in reasonable union. For instance, those who appreciate the arts, the theater and music move in the same circles; sports and racing enthusiasts find more in common with one another than with those whose entire lives are taken up with the championing of social and philanthropic causes. Associations among professionals and among those of similar interests and educational or social background are a natural manifestation of those personal affinities that are polarized by the law of attraction.

While natural levels do exist within society—the rich mingling with the rich and the poor with the poor—some, by talent and drive, are able to elevate themselves in the course of a generation from ignorance, poverty and lack of formal education to wealth, civic responsibility and educational achievement.

Then, there are the climbers who are forever striving to bridge the gap between their own social stratum and a supposedly higher one even as there are those who will positively not allow their castes to be penetrated. Obviously, such rivalry among status seekers produces clashes and struggles that cause interminable unhappiness in the world.

El Morya teaches that "the world's leaders in government, education and religion must understand the varying needs of men to play many roles in outpicturing life's total drama. The fact that all do not elect to be renunciates or monks or that all do not choose to seek romance and family responsibilities, in no way ought to steal the hopes that men and women may have to pursue a particular walk of life that experience requires. As they reach upward, either swiftly or moderately, each successive phase of personal and collective evolution serves the total evolving spiritual consciousness of the race, which must always rise out of the crucible of human thought and feeling by the power of divine alchemy into universal and individual Christhood."[2]

"How shall the world ever attain unity and compassionate peace if understanding does not become magnified by those who cherish brotherhood enough to sacrifice, if necessary, some portion of their own selfhood in order to externalize among men a required facet that will make up the central theme of illumined understanding in action. Life understood is more easily lived. Man when understood, is more easily loved with relish. God when understood, is the elevation of Self."[3]

When clubs and cliques prevent people from mingling in wider circles, people are prevented from expressing brotherhood in its broadest sense. But let us go a step further in our observations. First, we must acknowledge that brotherhood is the key to balancing personal and group karma. Then we will see that unless people determine to go beyond social barriers in their expression of brotherly love, they may hinder their own spiritual progress by depriving themselves of the opportunity to balance personal karma, race karma and national karma through world service.

Group Karma

Just what is race karma? What is group karma? And what is national karma?

When we speak of race consciousness, group consciousness

or national consciousness, we mean that, given a focus of attention (a football game, a national disaster or a triumph on the moon), large numbers of people can think, feel and act as one. Thus, we can easily see how the collective qualification of energy can produce collective karma.

For instance, in the case of mob violence, riot or revolution, individuals identify with a certain group or cause. When through their association with the group they bring about harm to society, to a town or to a community, they will have to balance their destructive acts as a group. They will, no doubt, be returned to embodiment as a group or be drawn together at a propitious time that they might be given the opportunity to render service to society as a group—perhaps through governmental, educational, cultural or religious institutions or through some joint philanthropic endeavor.

In such circumstances, there is both individual and collective responsibility. The individual can never blame the group for his actions; nevertheless, through his actions, he has tied himself both to the group and to those who have been wronged.

Expressions of Individuality: The Races

*And hath made of one blood
all nations of men for to dwell
on all the face of the earth . . .*

SAINT PAUL

Expressions of Individuality: The Races

OUR DISCUSSION OF BROTHERHOOD would not be complete without a consideration of the subject of race in light of individual and group karma.

When individuals act as a racial group, in the name of or on behalf of one race against another race, they incur race karma. Sometimes balancing race karma requires individuals or whole groups of people to embody in a race that is not native or otherwise necessary to their spiritual evolution. But because of the intense race hatred they have generated, they must return to the group toward which their hatred was directed to experience what it feels like to be on the receiving end of this energy.

For example, the akashic records reveal that one militant leader of the 1960s Black Power movement was, in a previous life, a cruel white taskmaster. Whereas his racial hatred was then directed with great vehemence against black slaves, this same hatred was, in this lifetime, directed against whites. Thus, we see that hatred manifests as substance misqualified within a person's world and like other human momentums, is carried over from one life to the next.

A focus of hatred in the electronic belt makes it possible for the forces of darkness to use that person to implement their schemes to undermine brotherhood. Among these dark forces there are no battle lines, no sides, no loyalties—only human pawns used to keep mankind enslaved through division and conflict.

Although knowledge of the origins and early development of the world's races is lost in the dim, unrecorded past, some men look to ancient and scriptural records to prove the superiority of one race over another and to justify their attitudes toward integration or segregation, as the case may be.

Some groups—and these may be found in all races— consider themselves underprivileged. These groups argue that history has held back their cultural development, and they take the position that the world owes them a living. Having no knowledge of karma, they do not see their own past actions as the cause of their present circumstances. In complete ignorance of the law of the circle, they transfer the blame for all their ills to society or to another race.

At the other extreme, there are those who champion a rugged individualism. They firmly believe that man must brave the world and work out his destiny (which is actually his karma) with a minimum of help from society. As long as this attitude does not stress the parable of the Good Samaritan[1] and the duty of being the keeper of one's brothers, it denies in part the need of nations and individuals to grow in grace and to work out their personal karma through service and ministration to one another.

We must consider the fact that social, political and racial theories can easily defeat not only the purposes of true brotherhood but also the law of karma. We must assess our own philosophies in the light of this higher criticism. Then, under the direction of our own Christ Self, we must determine which theories best serve the interests of man's individual spiritual development and the overall needs of a society seeking to bring in a Golden Age.

The Origins of Race

First, in the matter of race, let us study the writings of Chananda, a Master of the Far East and Chief of the Indian Council of the Great White Brotherhood.* In summing up the deliberations of the Darjeeling Council on this subject, he begins his statements with the remark: "Each day, man weaves a strand of his own future." Let us pause to consider this eternal truth, for it provides the key not only to the complexities of racial questions but also to our own existence.

"Each day, man weaves a strand of his own future." In this short sentence we come face to face with the realization that the individual is equal to the sum of his past plus the unknown quantity of his present drive as it is harnessed to the unlimited potential of the Christ. This will and this light can be used to transform the past, present and future of an individual's experience into the victorious life of a son of God.

Continuing his dissertation, Chananda says: "Long ago when the pigmentation of race was implanted in the soul structure of man through the radiation of the seven color rays,[2] there lived upon the planet what were known as the red man, the yellow man, the green man, the blue man and the purple man. At that time, the darker pigmentations of the skin did not exist.

---

*The Great White Brotherhood is a spiritual order of saints and adepts of every race, culture and religion. These Masters have transcended the cycles of karma and rebirth and reunited with the Spirit of the living God. The word "white" refers to the aura or halo of white light that surrounds them.

"Now, I am well aware of the fact that down through the years men have stressed the differences of race and that the brown and the black have been questioned in particular. But if individuals will think of themselves as solar manifestations of the living God—recognizing that the outer garment of race that they wear is only an overcoat that they will one day put off—they will cease to think of themselves as white, black, yellow, red or any other color.

"This attitude of mind is much to be desired. For while we cannot deny that racial prejudice does exist in the world—and that, without our favor—we propose, as one of the first steps to the shedding of the racial consciousness, that men understand who and what they are.

"Man is not his body any more than he is his memory, his emotions or his mind. He is a being. He has a body, he has a mind, he has a memory and he has a spirit. The spirit of man is neither black nor white: it is forever free. The consciousness of man and of his individuality is, however, very involved in his own density patterns. Men think black, they think white and they think yellow and red. . . .

"The problem lies not in the energy but in the vision of those who do not see the light that glows just beyond the veil of manifestation—who see only the limited release that passes through the form. The problem of density is not a problem of race; on the contrary, it is common to the whole human race. . . .

The Problem of Racial Conflict

"In matters of race, many have put themselves behind the eight ball. Evil dwells in all races; and wherever racial differences are given power in this uninhibited age, there is a strong possibility that violence and negative karma will accrue to the records of many lifestreams. We wish to avoid this most unfortunate eventuality, not only for the sake of humanity, but also for the sake of the individual.

"We know very well that a sharp thought or an unkind word can easily rise to the surface of the unguarded consciousness. But mankind should not indulge in a display of crassness concerning their own or another's race. After all, can the leopard change his spots? Can man by thinking add one cubit to his stature? As Christ said: 'The very hairs of your head are numbered.'[3]

"Man must learn to live not in his externals but in his internals and above all to keep the inside of his vessel spotlessly clean. Let all races heed this word, for it is an admonishment as well as an indictment. The furies released by mankind in racial disorders and riots, instead of putting forward the races that are behind, will put them further backward. And every individual who has augmented the strife by thought, word or deed—seen or unseen, known or unknown—will surely pay the penalty for all of the karma he has created. And this applies to both sides of the fence. . . .

"Man is a product of his environment, but he is also a product of his heredity. His heredity is twofold: (1) he has an earthly inheritance, a portion of which was bequeathed by his earthly parents, and another portion that represents his own karma from the present as well as past embodiments; and (2) he has a heavenly inheritance. His heavenly inheritance is the soul of God individualized and focalized for him as his very own I AM Presence and his Causal Body, which contains the solar fires he has magnetized through faith and good works.

"Each man possesses an infinitesimal drop of the ocean of infinity. He, himself, is intended to be a gatherer of more light as he makes his way along the homeward path and as the entire body of God expands throughout cosmos. As long as he limits himself to race, regardless of the sense of injustice he may have, he is actually selling his birthright for a mess of pottage. . . . [4]

"You cannot force people to love you or to accept you. You can only expand the light within your heart and by noble and useful effort, contribute to the well-being of the world community. If violence is to continue unabated in the world, it will be a long time before it comes to know the peace of Christ that passeth understanding. The hunger in the hearts of men and in the little children of all races for kindness and brotherly love clearly shows that if they could have their way, they would live together in harmony.

"The world must learn to live with what it cannot change and to change that which it can. Change can be wrought by the people of any race. I cite the miracle of George Washington Carver who, by his great love, won the respect of an entire nation. The son of a slave who, in one sense, was born in ignorance, achieved by his illustrious and noble spirit such freedom as few of any race have enjoyed.[5]

"Men must learn to garner respect first for themselves and for what they do. Then they must learn to respect the rights of others because they respect this freedom for themselves. Those who would expound upon nonviolence must be nonviolent in thought and in feeling as well as in word and deed. Mohandas K. Gandhi of our own land of India was a man of peace in every way. For this reason, he was successful in carrying out his campaign of nonviolence. Those who cry peace and safety but who are filled with violent feelings are hypocrites and traitors to Reality. They keep not the city of the world in peace, nor do they win by their efforts respect for their own race in the world community.

"Let those who would bring about a change in racial relations understand that all change begins within the individual. You can never legislate respect; you can only earn it. Among the white race, there are those who live in abject poverty and are looked down upon by many. These too can rise; for all can rise through their own noble efforts and put down the awful specter of violence that has loomed in the land and brewed destruction to the marvelous democratic principles upon which the nation America was founded. . . .

"May I remind you of the words of one of your American poets: 'We can make our lives sublime and, departing, leave behind us footprints on the sands of time.'"[6]

Root Races

Just as we see great variety in the races of man, so we find that there is also great diversity in the origin and soul evolution of the lifewaves currently working out their destiny on earth. According to esoteric tradition, seven primary groups of souls—the first to seventh root races—have been assigned to this planet. A root race is a lifewave, an evolution of souls that comes forth from the heart of God in a certain epoch in cosmic history to ensoul a particular ray. They share a unique archetypal pattern, divine plan and mission to fulfill on earth.

The first three root races lived in purity and innocence upon earth in three Golden Ages before the Fall of Adam and Eve. Through obedience to God's Law and total identification with the Real Self, the members of these three root races reunited with God through the ritual of the ascension. They lived in perfection in paradise. They did not descend into duality as good and evil but returned to God without ever experiencing sin.

The Fall of man that is described in allegory in the Bible took place tens of thousands of years ago on the ancient continent of Lemuria during the time of the fourth root race. Adam and Eve and many others, influenced by the fallen angels known as Serpents, chose to leave "paradise," which was a higher state of consciousness. By so doing, they became subject to the laws of karma and mortality.

Following the Fall, the fifth root race embodied. These were new souls who had never dwelt in flesh forms before and had never experienced the world of time and space. They came forth and copied the ways of those who were already in embodiment.

The sixth root race is a race of those who are destined to expand the Christ consciousness on the sixth ray. Theirs is a path of devotion, service and ministration. They began to take embodiment approximately two thousand years ago.

The fourth and fifth root races are those who were on Lemuria and Atlantis. They are older souls, who have embodied for the longest time on earth. They have the memory of ancient cultures and Golden Ages where Ascended Masters and Archangels walked and talked with men. They find it very easy to understand the personhood of God in his many emissaries.

The sixth root race are very young souls. As Jesus was the avatar who was sent in this age, he is the one they have seen and the one whom they follow. Because he is the only one they have known, it is difficult for them to acknowledge any other master.

Some members of the fourth, fifth and sixth root races are still in embodiment on earth today, and some of the sixth root race are yet to embody. The seventh root race is destined to incarnate in South America during the Aquarian age, the age of the seventh ray. They are being held back because the Lords of Karma do not wish to release these new souls, new lifewaves, to be once again contaminated by the ways of the old.

Each root race is sponsored by a Manu and his consort, who represent the Father-Mother God to their respective root races. The Ascended Masters teach that Manus ensoul the Christic image for the race they sponsor. In the Hindu tradition, the

Manus are the progenitors of humanity, the divine lawgivers.

In *The Secret Doctrine*, Russian-born mystic Helena P. Blavatsky says: "Orientalists and their dictionaries tell us that the term 'Manu' is from the root *Man* 'to think'; hence 'the thinking man.' But, esoterically, every Manu...is but the personified idea of the 'Thought Divine'...; each of the Manus, therefore, [is] the special god, the creator and fashioner of all that appears during his own respective cycle of being or Manvantara."[7]

The Manus of the fourth root race are Lord Himalaya and his divine complement. The Manus of the fifth root race are Vaivasvata Manu and his consort. The Manus of the sixth root race are the God and Goddess Meru.[8] The Manus of the coming seventh root race are the Great Divine Director and his divine complement.

The Unity of All Races through the Mother Flame

The Ascended Master Afra, who is the patron saint of Africa and the black race, teaches on the path of universal brotherhood. He spoke of this to the people of the African continent in a dictation delivered in Accra, Ghana, in 1976.

"Salutations in the flame of Afra! Let light flow unto a continent and unto a people! Let light flow from the fiery core of the I AM THAT I AM, from the side of the North unto the side of the South. Let the light descend from the crown unto the base. And let the fulfillment of the Father-Mother God be the reuniting of all peoples upon this continent. By the sacred fire of the Holy Spirit, let them be united in love under the banner of Micah, the angel of Unity, who also united the children of Israel and also united the people of America in time of civil war with the banner *Union* and with the cry, 'Remember ye are brethren.'[9]

"I call to the children of Afra. 'All your strength is in your union. All your danger is in discord.' So were the words of Hiawatha unto the tribes of the Indians.[10] And by the smoking of the peace pipe and the smoking of the lamps of God, the union of the sacred fire brought together the divergent tribes, and they became as one—one in the consciousness of God, one out of many, *e pluribus unum*.[11] So, one people out of many nations and origins and tribes.

"So as the individual yields to the family, as the family yields to the community, and as the community yields to the nation, let it be that in this hour of the coming of the Lord's Spirit in the descent of the fire of the Holy Ghost, the differences of the peoples of this continent shall be dissolved in the one flame of love. Let the gift of the Holy Spirit be the understanding of tongues—not only of the speech but of the heart and the mind and the soul.

"Let the people understand we are brethren because we are of the same Mother. Let Mother and the love of Mother be the flow. How can you kill when you kill the one who has come forth from the same womb of Mother? Out of the womb of the Cosmic Virgin, out of time and space you came forth as mighty conquerors, as teams of conquerors of old, as the blue race and the violet race. So you came and so you are one in the light of Alpha and Omega, the beginning and the ending, the first and the last, the one unity.[12] So, out of one, many; so, many is the coming of the one.

"I am your brother—not your lord, not your master, but I am your brother on the Path. I have shared your passion for freedom. I have shared with you the hours of crisis when you beheld injustice, when you sought the Lord and prayed to him for justice and the Lord gave to you the divine plan for this nation and for this continent.

"I have lived in your hearts these hundreds and hundreds of years as you have toiled under the burden of oppression from within and without. And although many have considered the outer oppression the greater, we who are among those who have graduated from this continent consider that the only true slavery is the slavery from within—the slavery of the carnal mind and its selfishness, its failure to sacrifice upon the altar as Abraham and Isaac sacrificed. So, the failure to sacrifice the beasts of the carnal mind: this is slavery.

"Now then, it is because some have been willing to make the sacrifice of selfishness that the outer slavery has also been broken, and it is the evolution of the people themselves toward the light of God that has given this new opportunity in this age to this continent."[13]

There are many tribes and races on the African continent, with a long history of conflict and bloodshed between them. Afra gave a vision of a common flame and dedication as the means to unity.

"I come, then, that you might see the great flow of the merging of the peoples in the river of the water of life that is the flow of Mother. In the crystal flow of Mother light from the base chakra to the crown of a continent, there is the merging of the people.

"And so as Mother Liberty came to the shores of America on behalf of her son Saint Germain to anoint the pilgrims who came to that land, to ignite in them the flame of the heart that they might be called the people of America—from every nation, from every origin, ethnic and racial, they came. They left behind their differences, they became one nation because Mother Liberty, standing in the harbor of New York, holding the torch high, kindled in their hearts that flame of oneness with the same message of the angel Micah: 'Remember ye are brethren. I AM your Mother; I have begotten thee.' This is what makes an American: it is a common flame, a common devotion, a common freedom."[14]

Thus, it is in the flame and the presence of the Mother that we find true brotherhood and unity. (This is a theme we shall explore in more detail in Section IV.) All of every race can give Afra's "Affirmations for Brotherhood":

> I walk in the footsteps of Afra.
> I AM a brother, a sister to all.
> I comfort. I console.
> I AM true to myself and to my God.
> I bear the honor of God in my heart.
> I enter into mystical union with the Holy Spirit.
> I AM one with the Prince of Peace.
> I shall walk in the Spirit from this day on.
> For this is the day of my victory.
> This is my hour and the power of light.
> I shall lead my people to the throne of Glory.
> Receive me now, O God!

Section III

Outlines on the Mirror of God Self-Awareness and the Family

For whosoever shall do the will of God, the same is my brother, and my sister, and mother.

JESUS

Outlines on the Mirror of God Self-Awareness and the Family

T<small>RUE BROTHERHOOD DOES NOT RE-</small>quire that an individual love the personal masks of his fellowmen, but rather that he see behind the many masks the one reality of God's own identity. The Divine One who gave a portion of himself to everyone (but remained inviolate as the Divine One) stimulates in all men the desire to manifest more and more of the fullness of life that lies just beyond the veil of the outer consciousness.

The mask is the human that we have to tear off so that the Divine can be manifest. But the Divine is so powerful that it shines through the mask and makes the mask beautiful and wonderful, so that we sometimes do not want to get rid of the mask, and we do not realize that its beauty is the Divine.

In reality, all that we have that is light and loveliness and beauty is the Divine. And if we want to attribute it to the mask, to the outer achievement, to the human, as so many do while they have youth and beauty and virility in life, we find that we are not dwelling in who we really are.

Removing the Mask

In *The Lost Teachings of Jesus,* we find an approach to the process of removing the mask of the human and identifying with the Divine Self.

"First of all, if we're going to take a mask off, we have to take the mask off of something. Now, what are we going to unmask? In this case, we must perceive that there is something Real about us; there is also something that is unreal about us. And the quicker we discover it and acknowledge it and learn to distinguish the difference, the quicker we will make progress in the light.

"Why is it important that we know the difference? It is important that we know the difference because otherwise we are going to be feeding the mask and starving the real man.

"Sooner or later you're going to bump into the very same mask you've created—only it'll be on someone else's face. It's the way the Law works: Like attracts like, and so in the caricature masks of others, you begin to recognize a few of your own eccentricities. Because, you know, you can't ever see yourself in the mirror as you really are.

"Even though the mask is unreal, you can't just say, 'Oh, it's not real,' and turn your back on it and ignore it. But there is one thing you can do. You can mock it!

"Therefore, in a sense, if we can learn to laugh at ourselves, we can actually break the ice of this frozen energy veil that prevents us from seeing our Real Self.

"There is also a serious side to removing the mask. And the serious side is that the divine creation, the wholly perfect creation of God, needs to be revealed by the unmasking.

"It is not just a matter of ridiculing our human ego—which in many cases has served us well and has helped us to discover many beautiful things about ourselves—because the ego is not all bad. In the initial stages of identity development, the ego represents the will to be. And the ego must have some sense of self-worth to maintain that will until the soul itself attains the strength and the desire for self-transcendence. At this point, the divine ego, magnetized by the soul's very will to be, supersedes the lesser ego—the lesser sense of selfhood no longer being needed to sustain the finite awareness.

"It is when the human ego becomes too rigid, too centered upon its own doings, that it becomes frozen in time. It doesn't move to the right or to the left. And this rigidity will be its ultimate undoing. In fact, its only chance for survival at that point will be its displacement by the divine filament of being.

"We may reach a point in this life, however, where everything becomes very brittle—and this is easy to do. And in the maturing process, which is intended to be an ennobling process, we sometimes lose sight of the goal—that is, we lose our balance and our perspective, and thus, we lose our way.

"When you come to a point where you desire to unmask yourself, this is not to belittle yourself. It's to get rid of the shell of illusion about anything—yourself or someone else.

"It is so important for us to learn that in removing the mask from the self, it's the Self we're uncovering—the *Real* Self. What we have to do is take the mask off of the Divine Presence and show the Divine—that which is shining through the mask. It is so powerful, so radiant that it shines through the mask!

"Realize that your God Presence has all the qualities of wisdom, all the qualities of compassion, all the qualities of peace, all the qualities of Christ-victory—every quality you need to make your ascension. If you will remind yourself that these qualities exist within the God Flame, if you'll fix that in your mind, this human person, the mask you see that is not real, will just simply fade away.

"You won't even have to take the mask off, because the mask will fade away. It'll perish! But in its place the spiritual flowers will grow in the garden of your heart."[1]

Right Association

When men see one another as impressions of the divine consciousness, outlines on the mirror of God's own Self-awareness, they are no longer confused by the distortions—the blurs—that men have made of the original image. Unmoved by the fluctuations of the ephemeral so-called selves that have raised themselves into positions of temporal power, the son of God who would be a healer of mankind and a catalyst for true brotherhood sees only the immovable identity of his fellowmen. He knows that this identity is preserved and hallowed in the mind of God. He knows what is real about his fellowmen, and it is the truth of the real identity to which he clings—no matter what the mortal manifestation may seem to be doing. This is the truth that sets him free to enter into a partnership with God that must eventuate in the manifestation of the brotherhood of man.

Men and women should not encourage association with those who are actively pursuing the downward path. Although Jesus was known as one who associated with publicans and sinners, his concern was for the freedom of the imprisoned soul. The great Hindu masters refer to one's fellowship with Truth and with those of like mind as *satsanga*. Unless there can be brought about through a relationship a mutual upliftment of consciousness or the spurring of the desire in the one on the downward path to find a higher life expression, involved relationships are best avoided.

Those who would manifest true brotherhood should seek to associate with those who are free from criticism, condemnation and judgment toward their fellowmen, with those who are not argumentative or motivated by the desire to strut the ego or to parade their ego-centered ideas. Rather should they pursue association with humble men and women who hold the sacred wisdom of God as a treasure of great price. They should likewise endeavor to manifest this treasure first, knowing that in so doing, all of the treasures of life shall ultimately be added unto them. "Seek ye first the kingdom of God, and his righteousness; and all these things shall be added unto you."[2]

The False Sense of Brotherhood

In their service to life, the members of the spiritual Brotherhood never base their expressions of friendship upon the modes of the outer, changing personal self. For they know that the magnetism of human sympathy is one of the chief causes of the perpetuation of a false sense of brotherhood. This false sense is based upon the tendency of the race toward gregariousness and the need for the approval of self and conduct by family and friends. When approval or favors are withdrawn, relationships are often terminated abruptly, revealing their flimsy foundations.

As Jesus proclaimed, "Whosoever shall do the will of my Father which is in heaven, the same is my brother, and sister, and mother."[3] So should his followers today in their service to life seek out and work with those who are following the Laws of God in their efforts to bring peace and brotherhood to the world. For it has been proved time and again that all attempts at cooperative endeavor with those whose moral standards are not grounded in the Laws of God, eventually fail.

Nonattachment

There is a great deal of self-love in the world. Most individuals, whether they admit it or not, are deeply and painfully attached to themselves. While this is understandable, it is not always desirable. For only in the ritual of detachment (or of nonattachment) is man free to identify with his own Higher Self and with the Higher Self of every other child of God.

Gautama Buddha taught that we should strive for nonattachment—to persons, places, conditions and things, as well as nonattachment to the fruits of action. We have to come to the place of desirelessness, of nonattachment, of having the desire, not to possess or to be possessed but to be one in the Flame of God. This is the test of selflessness. It is the overcoming of the propensity for attachment to one's self or to another person's self.

The Goddess Meru speaks of the necessity for nonattachment: "If, then, you would be free from these strings [ties of various sorts to other lifestreams on earth], which place you as a puppet, not of the Almighty but sometimes of the mass consciousness, you must come to the place upon the Path where you realize that the only state of consciousness is the state of nonattachment. Nonattachment to oneself is the greatest victory and the greatest freedom you can know.

"You do not even know how you are possessed of the carnal mind that still is within your own forcefield, how you are possessed by its desires, its longings, its attachments, its thoughts, its uneasiness, its inability to sit still or keep the thoughts and feelings still. This is bondage, precious hearts, and I proclaim it to you because I perceive that you know not that you are in a state of bondage because you have not divorced yourself from yourself. How, then, can you divorce yourself from the human consciousness of one another? But this you must do by recognizing that you must look up and live. Look up and live. Look up, I say, and live!

"You must look up into the face of your God Presence. You must behold that face day and night and sing the song of the new day: 'Holy, holy, holy, LORD God Almighty. Thou art holy in manifestation, in God and in man.'

"So then, when you determine to espouse the consciousness

of nonattachment, which precedes the consciousness of desire-lessness, you create a vacuum within your being, a vacuum that must be filled by God, his light and his abundance. When you desire nothing of this world but only to be God in manifestation, there is created a vortex around your being, a whirlwind action of the sacred fire. And from the four corners of the earth, from the four winds, comes to you the great quality of immortal peace, of blessedness, of abundance. All things are placed within your hand by the great River of Life, the great flow from the Almighty. For God will deliver unto you all that he holds dear for man when he sees that you will not desire to retain it, to possess it, but that you will allow that energy to flow through you in mighty torrents.

"See, then, the wealth, the health, the purity, the joy that bubbles in you as that bubbling brook in which you perceive the face of the Almighty. Then you will look and see and know when you perceive that image that God, in truth, is in manifestation in man, and you will notice that you are transformed. Even as you gaze upon the flesh form and see your mirrored image, you will see it no longer; you will look behind the veil and the mask of the actor in the play, and you will behold there the face of God."[4]

Personal Relationships as the Means to Develop Divine Love

The great world of spiritual reality can never be contained within the confines of one's personal self or the personal selves of others. Therefore, only when man can place himself outside of his own mask and outside of the masks of others is he able to understand the concept of true brotherhood.

Sentimentality is sustained because people are in love with themselves and with the image of themselves that they see reflected in others. Experiencing empathy with the unhappiness of others, they say, "There, but for the grace of God, go I." And often when these "others" suffer grave misfortune, they become martyrs in the eyes of the multitudes.

Earthly attachments based on jockeying for position by human egos can never produce the fruit of freedom. Such attachments do not lend themselves to a realization within the individual of the truth about man or real brotherhood. Such attachments are of human bondage, and without exception, they create ties that smother the development of the Real Self.

On the other hand, family situations and social contacts, when properly regarded, can be a means of developing divine love in the character. Those who practice the Presence of God in their lives can radiate service unto others that will give them tremendous assistance in developing their own divine nature.[5]

Even so, the Master Jesus has said, "A man's foes shall be they of his own household."[6] One wonders how those whom one cherishes the most can become one's enemies. Jesus' statement must be understood in the light of his knowledge of the treachery of the psychic forces of the planet. Working through one's closest and most trusted associates, these forces attempt to upset and unseat evolving souls. People do not expect their loved ones to betray them; therefore, loved ones become the best tools of the sinister force.

Be not dismayed, therefore, when those closest to you act contrary to your best interests. Instead, pray for their protection and hold them in the light of that same immaculate concept that God holds for them.

Confucius' Formula for Community

The foundation of true brotherhood is always the individual and the individual's relationship with God. This divine rela-

tionship is then extended to successively larger circles of awareness. Confucius, the great sage of ancient China, explained this
in his work, *The Great Learning*. Let us explore Confucius'
teaching as it relates to individuals, families and communities.
Here is the formula in Confucius' words:

"The ancients who wished to illustrate illustrious virtue
throughout the kingdom, first ordered well their own States.
Wishing to order well their States, they first regulated their
families. Wishing to regulate their families, they first cultivated
their persons. Wishing to cultivate their persons, they first
rectified their hearts. Wishing to rectify their hearts, they first
sought to be sincere in their thoughts. Wishing to be sincere in
their thoughts, they first extended to the utmost their knowledge. Such extension of knowledge lay in the investigation of
things.

"Things being investigated, knowledge became complete.
Their knowledge being complete, their thoughts were sincere.
Their thoughts being sincere, their hearts were then rectified.
Their hearts being rectified, their persons were cultivated. Their
persons being cultivated, their families were regulated. Their
families being regulated, their States were rightly governed.
Their States being rightly governed, the whole kingdom was
made tranquil and happy."[7]

Confucius has always been concerned with harmony and
divine order within the family as a unit of society. He was born
in 551 B.C. during a time of great turmoil and upheaval in
China. His father, an elderly soldier, died when he was three. In
the midst of social chaos in his country and the disorder in his
family from losing his father, we see the little boy Confucius
drawing Chinese characters in the dirt. We see his soul finding
consolation in the inner patterns of the Christ consciousness
and yearning to bring them out into the world.

Confucius dedicated his life to teaching others how to

bring order to one's self, one's family and to the empire. His teaching has been described as a social order in communion and collaboration with a cosmic order. Confucius believed we could bring order into our lives by tapping into the divine order of heaven and conveying its love and wisdom through culture and especially through ritual and music.

In this teaching, Confucius tells us that if we want to establish equanimity in our families and make them whole, we must first cultivate ourselves. Self-cultivation is becoming sensitive to the secret rays[8] as you develop them within yourself. When you cultivate the secret rays, you can attune to the etheric patterns, bring them into your life and empower your holy endeavors. The five secret rays are the high energy and power of the nucleus of life, the nucleus of your heart, the nucleus of the atom. They are the sheaths of the inner white-fire core of the atom.

The five secret rays form the core and essence of primary fire within you. And the primary fire is the fire of the heart. It is the blood of Christ. It is the manifest perfection of our Lord. This primary fire is within the secret chamber of the heart.

There are etheric patterns for our souls. There are etheric patterns for our families. And there are etheric patterns for our communities and in nature all around us. We can call to Confucius and other Ascended Masters to reveal and reinforce our etheric patterns so that these patterns may be our empowerment and guiding force. This is our call for divine order. Paul the Venetian has explained that just as a flower opens its petals according to its own preordained pattern, so we also blossom into our divine identity and destiny by getting in touch with and releasing our energies into our blueprint, or etheric pattern:

"Just as a flower joyously opens its petals according to its own preordained pattern, so man can release the energies of his consciousness into the blueprint of identity that marks the perfect concept and the patterned destiny—his very own from the beginning. Just as the etheric pattern of the flower is there—an electrical forcefield surrounding the bud with an aura of expectancy—so the design God has willed for each manifestation of himself surrounds the evolving monad as a cocoon of light, containing within itself all that man requires to fulfill his divine plan.

"As the flower unfolds, it follows the outline of the pattern that Nature has lovingly pressed upon its cellular structure. No resistance to the cosmic flow is here, but movement toward reunion with the Whole and a momentum of aeons, of life evolving life, begetting beauty and expanding the universal order. Thus Nature teaches man the Way; and if he would follow, his life, too, would be the outpicturing on earth of heaven's immortal loveliness."[9]

The Family as the Basic Unit of Society

As we seek to understand brotherhood as it manifests in the social order, let us begin with the family. The Aquarian age is the age of the divine family. We are at a point now where the age of the Divine Mother is coming into manifestation, and the Mother uniting with the Holy Spirit will manifest the Golden Age.

The feminine ray is the key to the realization of Father, Son and Holy Spirit in this plane. Without this Mother Flame, we would not have a polarity to draw down the action of the masculine ray that is anchored in Spirit.

The great purpose of love that is shared between two people, between bride and bridegroom, is so that they can experience the intensity of God's love as in the fiery core of Alpha and Omega and then make that love go forth and spread throughout cosmos. This is why when people are in love, they are inspired to write poetry and to do all kinds of creative things. The intensification of the action of the pink flame of love that becomes the ruby ray in the fiery core is a gift of God so that we may know how much he loves us, that we might know how much he loves the whole cosmos. This love that is shared becomes a fountain into which the bride and the bridegroom may continually dip in order to give it to all mankind.

Therefore, with love, with the sharing of love, one must love one's fellowman more. The stars must be loved more. The Ascended Masters must be loved more. God is loved with a greater intensity. Our purpose is loved more. If this is not the natural effect of love, then we can be certain that it is not divine love, because divine love must do this for the soul. The selfish love that wants to be apart and alone to dote upon itself rather than to give and give and give is a very dangerous love because it leads to the cancer of the very soul. True love is made manifest in the action of ministration and service, the sixth ray. Thus, marriage is the sacrament of the sixth ray.

El Morya has said that the reward for service is the opportunity for more service. The more you serve, the greater the pipeline of energy between you and God becomes. The crystal cord connecting you with your God Presence doesn't have to be only a fine thread. In the Golden Ages, the crystal cord was as large as the tube of light; man had unlimited power coming down from God as a waterfall of light.* He had so much power that when he misused it, he could create dinosaurs and all kinds of manifestations of darkness throughout the planet. Therefore, the Solar Logoi decreed that the crystal cord should be reduced in size. To prevent man's proclivity to do evil, the life force flowing through his crystal cord was reduced. This was done so that the Godhead would be releasing to mankind only that amount of energy sufficient to sustain life in the four lower bodies until mankind, by their own free will and their

---

*See The Chart of Your Divine Self, pp. 206–8.

own fiat, would determine to expand that flame to the glory of God in manifestation in man and in woman.

We can expand the crystal cord, and we can expand the threefold flame. We do this through service. The more we give, the more we increase the flow of energy from God to us. Therefore, love between two people is intended to be a magnet to magnetize more of God's love, more of his energy. Through this love, we can expand the forcefield of giving, and we can ultimately balance and expand the threefold flame and then increase the diameter of the crystal cord.

The Purpose of Marriage

After God created man and woman, he commanded them to "be fruitful and multiply and replenish the earth." And he made the immortal fiat, "Take dominion over the earth."[10]

This is the purpose of marriage: to take dominion over the earth; to be fruitful and multiply and replenish the earth. All that happens in the marriage circle is a part of this taking of dominion.

Marriage, then, is the sharing of life for the mastery of the energies of the self individually and as a unit. We must master planes of consciousness in order to be free of this round in time and space. In order to expand God, we must master our physical, emotional, mental and etheric energies.

There are a number of questions to consider when thinking of marriage. We must consider whether sharing a life with someone means that two together can accomplish more than the two separately. Can they harmonize their energies for a goal, for an ideal, for something more than simply living the good life and pursuing pleasure and the pleasure cult? If the answer is yes, there may be great value in the relationship. If the answer is no, then there is a question whether or not the relationship should be pursued.

When marriage is simply a platform for the pursuit of pleasure, it will wear out because the things of this world are transient and they do wear out. Marriages that are based on this foundation are doomed to failure. They are a waste of the opportunity to gain self-mastery.

There must be an overriding goal, a purpose, a vision, a dream that two people want to forge together. And this dream will override the elements of karma, the elements of opposition to the union, the discord, the petty things that come up in day-to-day living. Without vision, the marriage will perish. Each member of the marriage on earth must have a vision of what these two have come together to do as one.

Bearing One Another's Burden

The marriage ceremony itself is only a beginning. And when the vow is taken "for better for worse, for richer for poorer, in sickness and in health," this is a vow to share one another's karma. Each carried their karma on their own back; now it becomes a joint load. The weakness of one spouse is transmuted by the other's strength. That is what marriage is for—bearing a common load together.

As the karmic cycles unfold and there is sickness and there is hardship, we realize this is what we have agreed to share. We have experienced the beauties and the joys of marriage; we must also share the unwinding of karma as it comes all through life. And even this can be shared in bliss if we use the violet flame together each day. And we do need to use it daily, because each day there will be a new allotment of energy. As Jesus said, "Sufficient unto the day is the evil thereof"—sufficient unto the day is the release of karma.[11] Each morning at dawn there is that day's release of karma, of energy with which we must deal. If we transmute it together and put our common energies into the common flame, we can go forward in creativity throughout the day and make the most of our sharing.

Twin Flames and Soul Mates

The real understanding of relationships and the intense longing for wholeness that often spurs them goes back to the very origin of life and the creation of individual Spirit sparks—twin flames that formed a single white-fire body, then separated out to manifest two spheres of being in polarity: masculine and feminine.

Each sphere became a body of First Cause, or Causal Body. The Spirit sparks became the focus of each I AM Presence, from which twin souls descended to begin their evolutionary rounds in the various dimensions of the Spirit-Matter Cosmos.

Whereas twin flames are one in Spirit and in their spiritual origin, soul mates are souls sharing a complementary calling in life. They are mates in the sense of being partners for the journey, co-workers, very much alike and very compatible because their initiations on the path of soul development are at the same levels but in polarity. They work well together, are project oriented, well mated and often have similar facial features and physique.

Twin flames share a destiny beyond the stars, are bound in eternity by the Holy Ghost and are never separated—though they may be kept apart physically by circumstance for centuries. The mind, heart and consciousness of twin flames flow from the same fount. But soul mates are companions in the schoolroom of life, and there may be a number of such associations in the history of the soul's evolution through the rounds of rebirth.

FIGURE 1: The Creation of Twin Flames

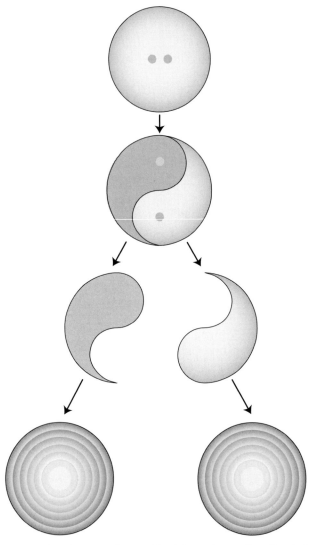

Representing the masculine and feminine polarity of God's wholeness, the T'ai chi rotates and divides into two identical spheres—twin flames of the One. A drop from the ocean of God's being, each sphere, or Divine Monad, consists of the I AM Presence surrounded by the spheres (rings of color, of light) that comprise the Causal Body. In this way, the Father-Mother God created us in their own image—male and female.

Each I AM Presence then sends forth a ray—a soul. Each soul focuses the opposite polarity—one, masculine; the other, feminine. Between the soul evolving on earth and the I AM Presence stands the Christ Self—our personal Mediator between Spirit and Matter.

Karmic Marriages and Relationships

The encounter that produces a spiritual polarity and an intense mutual love between individuals can be the result of many different circumstances. As well as the tie of twin flames and soul mates, there is also the bond of karma, and the karmic tie may be the tightest of all.

Because it is not free, it is binding. Because it is not balanced, the internal harmonies are wanting. And from time to time, there is an emptiness, a loneliness, that reveals the inadequacy of a relationship based solely on karma.

We may have several such relationships with people with whom we have made karma in our past lives—good karma and bad karma. Sometimes the worse the karma, the more intense the impact when we first meet someone, because there is God—the God we ourselves have imprisoned through past negative activity—and we run to greet that one to set them free from our own past transgressions of their being. And we love much because there is much to be forgiven.

A negative experience of the past—such as violence, passionate hatred, murder, noncaring for one's children, one's family, something that you have been involved in with someone else that has caused an imbalance both in their lifestream and in yours and perhaps in the lives of many—is experienced as a weight upon the heart and an absence of resolution at the soul level. This is a very gnawing condition that troubles the consciousness until it is resolved by love.

Your soul knows why you have come into embodiment. You have been told by your spiritual teachers, your Christ Self or guardian angel: "There is this situation with this individual that requires resolution. You and this person, by neglect, by your failure to act, once caused the collapse of this city, or because you walked away from your responsibility, many people were involved in a famine."

These are not unlikely situations. The ramifications of what we do by committing sin or by omitting to serve life are very great, and they are very heavy. At inner levels, the soul who is on the Homeward path (going home to the Father-Mother God) is very conscientious and desirous of righting the wrongs of the past—because the soul knows that righting the wrongs of lifetimes of ignorant and erroneous sowings is the only way to get back to the place we started from.

You must realize that you are going to meet such people, but the meeting of such a person is by no means the sign of an enduring alliance in the Christ. It is a sign that you are on the way back to God, that you have karma to be balanced. It is far better if you can get through the balancing of this karma without getting into the old spirals and the old creations of misuses of the sacred fire again.

Such a meeting can be like the impact of planetary bodies. It may be stunning because at the subconscious level you are elated that you have found the person with whom you can balance a certain record of karma. Your soul knows that if you do not get through that karma, you cannot go on to the next slice of the spiral of life and then on to world service and the creative projects you want most to do with the one you love most—even though you may have never met.

When you encounter such an immediate attraction to another person, it is always wise to determine: "I am going to meditate upon the flame, call for the violet flame for the transmutation of past karma and really work at this. And once I have done my invocations over a certain period of time, then I will see if there is anything left of the relationship." If you can do this, many times you will find that the relationship has dissolved before it was even made, and you have saved yourself agony, heartbreak and the making of more karma.

If you really want light in a relationship, test it by letting the violet flame blaze through the energy. Do not think that an instant attraction is a sign from heaven that you have met your twin flame or your soul mate. Magnetic attractions are the polarities of our karma.

On the other hand, there are ties of positive karma, and you may find that a Master may have told you before you took embodiment in this life that because of the many constructive labors for humanity you have done together, you are assigned an even greater responsibility with this person in this life. And because of your good karma, you will be happy and fruitful and have many victories for the Right.

In this time of our souls' acceleration toward Aquarius, we may experience more than one relationship of either positive or negative karma. We are winding up the loose ends of our karma with a number of people. These equations of our karma can cause distress, divorce, soul-searching and a real need to understand why our lives have not followed the perfect storybook pattern. The knowledge of karma and reincarnation can teach us a great deal about the bumpy road of relationships: some beautiful and some unpleasant—but all very necessary to the soul's evolution and the path of defining our true selfhood with God, Christ and our twin flame.

The way to get to a place where you marry either your twin flame or your soul mate is to pursue your meditation on the violet flame and clean up the energies of karma that have in the past been the forcefield of magnetic attraction, of instant attractions on a sensual basis. If you clean up those forcefields in your electronic belt by meditation, by application to the violet flame, you will clear away the debris that will make for an unwholesome alliance in the world.

You will find that gradually it is no longer the pull of the senses or the pull of karma that attracts you to people. It will be the pull of spiritual energies—the pull of a common flame, a common devotion. And before you realize it, you find that you are in polarity with a person on the basis of spiritual light, and it makes all the difference in the world, because that spiritual light is enduring. It can endure the ups and downs and coming and going of sexual satisfactions or the pleasure of the world or all of the things of this world upon which most marriages are based.

Marriage and the Family Are Ordained by God

Marriage is the most sacred union upon earth. It commemorates, firstly, the union of the soul with the I AM Presence. Secondly, it commemorates the union of twin flames. The goal of the soul is to find God first, because in finding God, there is something to bring to the twin flame.

The Goddess of Purity is a great being of light who holds a flame of purity for earth and her evolutions. She has explained the importance of marriage in God's plan for man and his spiritual evolution: "I would teach you, precious hearts who have prayed to the Lords of Karma for an understanding of the proper and true relationship of man and woman. For you must understand that the Lord Maha Chohan and the entire Spirit of the Great White Brotherhood desire to sponsor the Holy Family as the foundation for the Aquarian age and the bringing in of the seventh root race.

"Therefore, you must understand that the laws pertaining to marriage and the association of man and woman upon this planet were established by the Hierarchy as a manifestation whereby individuals who find that the flame of love glows between them, as the flame of the Holy Spirit and the spark of Alpha and Omega, might commit themselves to one another in true love for the creativity of the fires of God to bring forth not only children but also the building blocks of Reality, designs of the Holy Spirit, the industry of the Godhead; and thus, hand in hand move together in life, representing the Father-Mother God in the activity of their choice, in the calling and the election they have made their own.

"Thus, God gave to Adam an helpmeet, and Eve was born and taken out of the rib of Adam.[12] Thus, woman comes forth to adore and adorn the Masculine Ray of the Spirit, which she must uphold as the fire within the heart of the one who represents to her the husband as the maker of herself.[13]

"Thus, long ago to curb man's carnality, the Karmic Board did establish the custom of marriage and the laws of marriage, whereby through a representative of the Church, individuals who should come forth and present themselves as desiring to be made one in the Flame might receive the blessing of the Christ through the hand of priest or priestess at the altar of God.

"These laws have not changed, and whereas freedom is the flame that blazes in the Aquarian age, that freedom can never be interpreted as license for premature relationships and abuses of the sacred fire that are not in keeping with the Law. For the fire that is used in the relationship, the communion with the Holy Ghost, the supreme moment of bliss between man and woman must be sealed by commitment, by responsibility, by law and by blessing.

"Thus, the fiat went forth as a blessing upon twin flames, 'That which God hath joined together, let not man put asunder.'[14] Thus, the original and true marriage is with the twin flame. It is a marriage of the Flame of God and the Flame of God—of those two portions of the divine Whole that make up the complement of father and mother.

"Through karmic experience, through evolution, through departure from the Laws of God, twin flames have become separated. While some walk the earth, others are in temples of light in the etheric plane. Some are separated by age. Others are separated geographically because of the exigencies of their karmic circumstance. Thus, it has been declared by Hierarchy as an acceptable mode for man and woman to come together who are not necessarily twin flames but who desire through mutual service, because of their mutual karma, to walk together in an embodiment in the service of the Christ.

"And thus, there are marriages that are made in heaven by God, which is the marriage of twin flames, and there are marriages that are made upon earth through the commitment of souls to one another. And this is also ordained by God with his blessing, for did he not say, 'Be fruitful and multiply and replenish the earth.'

"Thus, in the presence of purity, man and woman learn the correct use of the sacred fire and how they must dedicate these energies to the divine union in the Holy Spirit and how, until they attain that union that is acceptable to God and man, they must garner these energies in the chakras for the creativity that is also an opportunity for mastery in the focalization within one body, one mind and spirit of the androgynous nature of the Godhead. Thus, in holy orders where men and women elect to take the vow of celibacy, the Holy Spirit assists them in maintaining the cosmic flow through the androgynous energies of the Alpha to Omega spiral.

"Both ways are acceptable unto the Godhead, and there are some who are made eunuchs in heaven, who are born to focus that flame. There are some who desire to make themselves eunuchs of men. These are those who feel that calling and desire to make that commitment.[15] And then there are those who have consecrated themselves at inner levels to the bringing forth of the children of the Most High God.

"You must understand, precious hearts, that the uses of the sacred fire for the bringing forth of children are sacred before the tabernacle of God. The use of this energy has always been sacred, and thus, there is no shame, as Saint Paul said, in the marriage state, for it is and was ordained by God.[16]

"You must understand, then, that all of the forces of darkness, all of the angels of Lucifer, of the Liar and his lie, have stood before the Divine Mother to tear down the virgin consciousness, to tear down the sacred-fire energies, and to strut before mankind the misuses of the sacred fire, the degradations of that temple of the Holy Spirit. This does not make the exchange of the sacred fire unholy, but it is an attempt to place before your gaze the image of unholiness, of sacrilege, so that you will lose the flame in disgust and refrain from the responsibilities, the joys, the bliss, the opportunity of the marriage state.

"Let all know, then, this day that the Lords of Karma proclaim the opportunity to these who desire to sponsor the seventh root race that in purity and in surrender heaven extends to you its honor, if you will extend to heaven your honor and be willing to accept the responsibility of the Holy Family, the Trinity of Father and Mother and Son, which culminates in the manifestation of the Holy Spirit."[17]

We will discuss the concept of "free love" in more detail in a future chapter of the *Climb the Highest Mountain* series. Let us say here only that when people indulge in premarital relationships, most sexual involvements are simply an exchange of energies at the electronic belt level. They take on some of the electronic belt patterns of their partner, and these remain with them. (Whereas, within the circle of marriage and its sealing in the Trinity, there is the opportunity through spiritual attunement and the raising up of energies through meditation, for there to be an exchange through all of the chakras of the great Causal Body—the great spheres of cosmic consciousness.)

The consciousness of free love and moving in and out with people is a challenge to the union of Father-Mother God in all endeavors. It is a challenge to the Holy Family that is the foundation of the Aquarian age.

Opposition to the Family

We must consider how all of the ravages of darkness are working together to tear apart the family and the family ideal in our society. We are all aware of the symptoms of the besieged family—high divorce rates, teenage pregnancy, increased welfare, rising crime and drug abuse, battered wives, child abuse, and so on. We must consider that this opposition must mean that the crux of family life—in it the very evolution and continuity of life on the planet—is at stake.

Divorce is often caused because partners who may be very well-suited to one another are not willing to sacrifice individually for the good of the unit. People can tend to be selfish, and we tend to expect too much from our mates. We tend to feel that if everything is not perfect in a marriage, the whole thing should be dissolved.

Whatever comes between father and mother as discord, will stop the flow of the Holy Spirit. Your life is no longer your own when you are married and have a family. You are constantly serving, constantly giving. And marriages break up because someone stops giving—someone stops wanting to give.

There may be situations where divorce is appropriate. Although the Masters have never approved divorcing a spouse on the basis of simply tiring of a plaything or finding a better sexual partner, the Brotherhood understands that in one lifetime we are expected to balance many areas of karma, and some of these conditions of karma can only be balanced through marriage. And so, for partners in a karmic marriage, at the end of that marriage, whether it's two years or fifty years, the karma is satisfied, and one repolarizes oneself back to God, back to the origin, back to the twin flame, back to service to the Brotherhood.

The Brotherhood tells us that each one must search his soul and discover whether or not he has done all in his power to bring harmony to a marriage and a home, to make a go of it, and whether there is such disagreement and such discord that it would be more costly to the partners to remain together than it would be to go their separate ways.

We have a society that rushes into marriage and thinks of marriage as the solution to all of one's problems. People are not spiritually educated for marriage, as to its spiritual significance as the sixth sacrament on the Path. And so, people are often very immature when they marry, and they come to the conclusion a number of years later, that it was not the right step.

The Ascended Masters are concerned that you do not walk out on your responsibilities and your karma. It is a very private matter between you and God. We have to beware of self-righteousness in marriage, of condemnation of the spouse. We have to beware of intolerance. Our spouses do not have to be the same religion as we are. They may be very devout and holy people in their own vein.

What is important is that there be harmony, and if there are children in the family, that they see a unity of the parents, a proper and dignified representation of the Father-Mother God and not continual strife and self-degradation.

When two people are making more karma together than they would be apart, it is a lawful reason to consider that a divorce should take place.

Children in the Family

One of the great joys and purposes of marriage is to bring forth children who can carry on in their mission, even as through them we are allowed to fulfill our mission. It is wise to respect the opportunity God gives us to bear children and to rejoice in the opportunity of giving life to those from whom sometime, somewhere we may have taken life.

Children do not always represent karmic debts that we are paying off, but more often, children are specific souls with whom we have karma. Sometimes parents who have already had children and have balanced the karma they are intended to balance in this life through childbearing, may then be chosen by God to bring forth children with whom they have no negative karma. These may be highly gifted children who may make a great contribution to society by bringing back their past attainment with them.

Every child who is conceived has a divine plan and a divine design. When these children are denied opportunity to come into embodiment through abortion, the divine plan of the soul is aborted. And when, through doctrines of population control, through sterilization or through abortion, parents do not bring forth the children they are destined to in this life, not only is the opportunity to balance that karma denied, but even the spiritual ecology of the planet is affected.[18]

When you are fully prepared to be a parent, the divine mate will be brought to you so that you can bring in the right souls. It is very important to prepare yourself for this high calling and to keep your light and your energy contained within you. It takes a certain forcefield of Christ consciousness within your aura to attract the Christ as a polarity. You cannot attract to yourself what you are not. All the wonderful things you want in a life's partner, you must have within yourself as a polarity. You want all that is real about yourself to manifest in your life's partner, and you must consciously invoke those qualities and hold them in your heart.

The Golden Age of the Family

Lady Master Nada explains the importance of the family as we seek to establish a Golden Age of Aquarius. "As the Hierarchy observes the present plight of mankind—the dilemma of personal and planetary karma—and as Hierarchy is concerned for mankind's transition into the Golden Age, Hierarchy looks forth to individuals nourishing the flame, the threefold flame of life, as anchoring points for the energies and the spirals of a new age.…

"The Aquarian age is also known as the golden age of the family, for it is through the matrix of the family that Hierarchy will allow sons and daughters of God to balance the energies of their karma. This matrix of the Holy Family, which was founded by Mary and Joseph and Jesus as the Trinity of Father, Mother, Son (and Holy Spirit as the flame ensconced in the three), is a matrix that does not exclude the way of the celibate, the way of priest and priestess of Holy Orders. The matrix of the divine family is for the nourishment of souls waiting to be born to release the sacred fire of the golden morn into form, into the here and now for the healing of the nations and for the healing of the planes of Mater.…*

"Therefore, as I am sponsoring, as a member of the Karmic Board as well as the chohan of the sixth ray, souls waiting to be born, I come forth, then, with a proclamation and the initiation of the spiral of this Golden-Age family to fulfill the fiat of Saint Germain, to fulfill the initiation of light from the heart of Alpha and Omega, and to nourish love and wisdom and power in hearth and in home."[19]

---

*Mater: Latin for "mother." Mater is the *mater*-ialization of the God Flame, the means whereby Spirit acquires, 'physically', fourfold dimension and form through the feminine, or negative polarity of the Godhead. The term used interchangeably with "Matter" to describe the planes of being that conform to and comprise the universal chalice, or matrix, for the descent of that light of God that is perceived as Mother.

As we look at the Holy Family of Joseph, Mary and Jesus, we see that Saint Germain (who was embodied as Saint Joseph) and Mother Mary were not twin flames but soul mates. They had a certain mission to accomplish, a certain attainment they had to manifest in that life. Both of their twin flames were ascended. Mother Mary is the twin flame of Archangel Raphael, and Saint Germain is the twin flame of Portia, the Goddess of Justice.

Raphael and Portia were in cosmic spheres in the highest level of God consciousness; and therefore, this tremendous polarity of their beings enabled Mary and Saint Germain to have access to their cosmic consciousness and to bring the fruit of the individual Causal Bodies of their twin flames into the manifestation of the founding of the Christian dispensation and the bringing forth of the Christ.

As we seek to outpicture the matrix of the Holy Family in our own lives, we can ask Mother Mary and Saint Germain to guide us and assist us as we hold the office of father or mother in our own families.

Scenes from the Life of the Holy Family

Saint Germain shares with us some of his experiences as Saint Joseph, the father of Jesus: "I disciplined Jesus that he might fulfill the Law and the way of the Christ. Oh, you did not know that it was necessary to discipline Jesus? You thought, perhaps, he was just born a lightbearer and perfect all his life. Well, I tell you that these things are deleted from scripture to make him an exception to the rule. And those of you who bring forth children of the New Age must understand that it does not matter the inner attainment of the Christ, the outer self must be disciplined, because it has a tie and a magnetism to the world outside that is based on self-indulgence.

And therefore, the child must be trained. The child must be trained as chela from birth and not indulged in the ways of the world. And this is the meaning and the purpose of Joseph coming to care for Mary and the Child."[20]

Mother Mary has also given glimpses of her life as the mother of Jesus, and of the joys and challenges of holding the flame for the Holy Family and for Jesus' mission. "In olden days, it was my joy to contemplate the mastery of my son, Jesus. Today all of the children of the world are regarded by me as my own. And when one of them reaches up heart, head or hand in divine seeking or yearning to serve the kingdom come, I cannot fail to respond to that one if I am called upon.

"If beloved Jesus came to me as a small child and he had been wandering about in bramble bushes, and thorns had pierced his feet so prematurely, I removed those thorns. And I would remove the thorns of life from the pathway of men today with as much happiness as I served my own son in that segment of history."[21]

"With God all things *are* possible. And these blessed words are a great hope to the present and coming age. And they are also my hope for each one of you, for men and women of every race, dwelling in every clime, as citizens of every nation. The cradling of a Christ was never enough in itself, for I gloried in the joy of observing his growth year by year, watching him stretch his tiny limbs and at last seeing him running forth in youth, maturity and then Christhood!"[22]

"It was a delightful day whenever I noted some particular God-quality that I wished to manifest in the boy Jesus blossoming in full flower within his gifted world. Oh, I knew full well that the buds were there, that the flame upon his heart's altar was kindled from on high and that he willed to do whatever would be revealed to him as the Father's will. Yet, I could not escape delight in seeing the unfoldment of each tiny change, effectively readying him for the arduous days ahead.

"Likewise, I wait with patience and love the unfoldment of that wonderful life radiance that beats your hearts. I wait for all men to be as free as beloved Jesus became."[23]

"I saw him in infancy, when the holy gleam of mission brought forth the radiance of unperceived wonder in his tiny eyes. I watched as through the years the flame of illumination and the communion ray from the heart of God changed that look into maturity and the confidence of a master of men and above all, of himself. I saw the rude multitudes utter blasphemies against his purpose. I watched from time to time with, I must confess, some trepidation, as threats were made against his life, as they sought to stone him or to push him over the side of a cliff.

"Lest some of you think it not befitting that I should confess my concern, let me recall for you that this was a period of great testing prior to my ascension. It was a time when I was both a devotee of some spiritual attainment and a mother of a living son, issued forth from my own womb.

"I cite this instance not to weaken your faith in my efforts in the name of God, but that you may no longer chide yourselves for those human weaknesses that are so much a part of the struggle. For one day, these too shall cease, as your hearts are finally schooled in the mastery of the aggressive suggestions of the world as well as in the mastery of yourselves."[24]

"I recall one morning when beloved Jesus was yet a small lad that he came to me with a very hard piece of wood that he was trying to whittle. He desired that I should persuade Joseph to exchange it for a softer piece, one that would lend itself more easily to molding. I set him on my knee, and I proceeded to explain to him that there was an ingrained quality that of old had been placed within the tree making one to possess a harder quality and another a softer quality. I told him that the soft wood would easily mar and that, were he to use it, the little image that he sought to whittle would not endure the knocks and tumbles that might later come to it, whereas a carving made of hard wood would endure more substantially.

"I also told him that the wood enjoyed being shaped by his hands and that the only difference between the soft and the hard wood would be that of a greater use of patience on his part. He brushed back his hair, which had fallen across his eyes, and with great and quick gentleness, planted a kiss upon both of my cheeks. I noticed a trace of a tear in one eye as he dashed away to continue his work of shaping the hard wood."[25]

Opposition to the Child

The God and Goddess Meru hold the focus of the feminine ray of the planet in their retreat over Lake Titicaca in the Andes Mountains of Peru. They are the Manus, or sponsors, of the sixth root race of incoming souls and are concerned with the protection and education of these souls.

God Meru speaks to us of the forces directed against the youth of the world and the burdens they face, even leading to suicide: "They are the target in every nation through all the world of the forces of Death and Hell. And those who are adults seldom comprehend what burdens lead the teenager to suicide. These are not all nonthinking ones. Some simply fall beneath the weight of their cross, bearing as they do a portion of world karma. For they have volunteered before taking embodiment, and there has been no Simon the Cyrenian to carry that cross for them while they should also bear the karma of the earth—no Joseph of Arimathea to anoint their bodies with myrrh and aloes.

"There are Christed ones in the earth, and Mother Mary

has called the Messenger and does call you now—'Take them down from the cross!' This is the message that comes from the heart of the *Pietà*.

"Realize that the Divine Mother in you must understand that the gap called the generation gap is that which is perpetuated by demons and false hierarchies of anti-youth in the earth. And they move to separate you from sensitivity to the situation and seeing the problems or knowing just how far a child, a teenager may be dragged into the grips of the toilers of the astral plane.

"They [children and teenagers] do not tell you, for they would keep up the appearance of that which you desire to see, ever desiring to please the parent. Thus, in so doing, they forfeit any assistance that might be forthcoming—and then it is too late and too hard to bear."[26]

A Plan for the Youth of the World

In these times, there are great burdens on families, children and youth. In assessing these situations, the God and Goddess Meru have evolved a plan for the cooperation of the child, the family and the community. Meru says: "I read to you now a scroll. This scroll has been penned by the angels of our retreat. And it is the setting forth by the beloved Goddess Meru and myself of the priorities that we see for the protection and the securing of youth to a ripened age of maturity and Christhood at thirty-three:

"First and foremost, *the dedication of education upon the Word and the Sacred Heart*—dedicating the three R's as the three rays of the threefold flame and therefore, setting the foundation whereby all learning might proceed from within....

"Parents need understanding and training. Therefore, second on our list is *parental training....*

"There must be as point three *a pact* made *twixt parents, teachers and sponsors of children* to work together as a three-fold flame of devotion in this community and then city by city. This entails the realization that Death and Hell desire to devour your children, and therefore, you must pray fervently! You must vow, after understanding the meaning of the vow, to stand between the youth of the world and Death and Hell....

"Fourth on our list must be the white-fire bastion of *the vow* made.... Once the vow is taken, you must remember the first Mother of the Flame, Clara Louise, who kept a daily prayer vigil for the youth, beginning at four in the morning and not concluding till late morning, praying for all souls of the youth, from the unborn to those in college and beyond....

"*Community action* is next on our list—an involvement of community that does reinforce family as these twin pillars of family and community brace a path of individualism for those of all ages. The breaking down of the family, the breaking down of the neighborhood communities—this is a fragmenting of society and the separation of members of karmic groups as well as individuals of varying ages so that they cannot learn from one another and ripen and mature, as the mature inspire those coming up, and the youth introduce the new wave of a New Age that can also challenge those in the middle of life or retiring.

"Community, then, must be a stronghold of values, of serving together, of meeting one another's needs and of establishing goals and priorities, not the least of which is the protection of that circle of lives. Blessed ones, a community must have more than the survival of itself or its happiness as a goal. It must have a totality of a reason for being toward which every member is galvanized and does rise.

"Apropos this, our next point on the list is the *training* of all members of society, and especially the children, *in responsible citizenship*—in taking responsibility for the necessary functions of the group, whether as a police force, as firemen, as a city council or as those who are supplying the unguent and the service in order that a community might endure.

"When all of the forces of chaos are attempting to break down a way of life, let us turn to *the music of the spheres*. Let us turn to the quieting of souls, to the invoking of harmonies, to the bringing forth of the Golden-Age sounds that have not been heard. Thus, this point on our list is an activation from the heart of Cyclopea, who does join us in sponsoring this call. Cyclopea holds secret melodies waiting to come forth that will remind the youth of ancient times, inner vows, other years when beauty and love, even in etheric octaves, was their lot.

"The youth need comfort of the Holy Spirit and not surfeiting. Tragically, tragically, few among them in actuality desire a path and a discipleship. Therefore, we do recommend the study and the structuring of a program that does *reinforce individuality* and thereby diminish the necessity in perilous times for such an emotional interdependence among teenagers as to make them fear to stand their ground for a cause or a principle.

"Why is peer pressure of such great consequence, beloved? Is it because of absence of parental reinforcement, understanding and even the camaraderie of a family that is not so distant and that does not set artificial barriers between one generation and the next? Let us not so poorly educate children as to see that they do not know their own minds or hearts or values, having had no noble ideals or stories of saints and heroes or examples of karmic consequences of misdeeds. . . .

"We are the God and Goddess Meru. We are the sponsors and the teachers of Jesus and all who have come to minister unto the sixth root race. Thus, Jesus and many other saints have long studied in our retreat. It is a home base for them. We invite you to come frequently. . . . Thus, you know that with the World Teachers we shall abide with you until every child on earth does have the opportunity to be tutored in the heart by the Holy Christ Self and by anointed teachers and parents and sponsors."[27]

Section IV

"I and My Mother Are One"
The Mother Flame

Honour thy father and thy mother:
that thy days may be long
upon the land which
the LORD thy God giveth thee.
EXODUS

"I and My Mother Are One" The Mother Flame

Every member of the Great White Brotherhood is a devotee of the Universal Mother, because Mother is the one who can be all things unto all people. She assumes the highest and the lowest manifestation of God, and in seeing her, we can understand the perfect posture of our being in each and every moment of our life.

Mother is our Guru and our teacher because of this very quality of flow. The fluidity of her presence heals us of brittleness, heals us of self-idolatry, heals us of all those things that are but fragmentary perceptions of the Path. When we see Mother, we see and understand perfect love. We understand how we ought to walk and talk with one another and how we, too, can bank the fires of the heart so that the fire is ready for the melting of those elements of the fragmented soul. When we see Mother, we understand that we, too, can be within our very souls a wellspring of life. The rising ascension flame is the cup of living water we give as Mother in Christ's name.

Let us celebrate Mother as the universal resolver of every

problem, every illusion, every fantasy, every fragmented and broken heart or broken life. Let us understand who is Mother.

God is Mother.

Let us not raise up an idol in her place. Let us worship together her living Spirit.

At certain times there comes a dispensation when God as Mother comes to the fore in incarnation through the Mother Flame. This Mother Flame is in all of us, and there have been a number of representatives of the Divine Mother on earth through many thousands of years. When the fullness of Father, Son and Holy Spirit has been transferred through the Law, through the interpretation of the Law in the teaching, and through demonstration of the miracles of the Holy Spirit, then there is the time for the coming of the religion of the Mother.

El Morya explains: "When activity is guided by the will of the Holy Mother, then the banner of the Mother of the World unfolds and heralds brotherhood everywhere—but it is a brotherhood of illumination, not a brotherhood of darkness or of self-aggrandizement. It is a brotherhood of givingness, and the abundant life is shared by all."[1]

The culmination of the brotherhood of man under the Fatherhood of God is found in the Mother Flame.

Mary the Mother

Mother Mary is one representative of the Divine Mother. She is the feminine counterpart of Raphael, the Archangel of the Fifth Ray. Their retreat is in the etheric octave over Fátima, Portugal—hence her appearances there. She descended to earth and in her incarnations on this planet kept the flame of our Christhood all the way from the healing temples of Atlantis to the Holy Land, where she embodied as the mother of David, and finally the mother of Jesus.

She fulfilled the purpose for her descent and did then ascend back to the heart of God. Having lived in human form, having lived at the side of our Saviour, she knows our needs, our burdens. In her, God as Mother is complete and perfect; and there are also many other Lady Masters in heaven.

Mother Mary's message to the world is not only for Catholics. It is the universal message of the universal Woman Clothed with the Sun, and it is given to every lightbearer on earth of every religion or no religion. You may appeal to her as the best part of yourself, as the mighty angel of God that she is.

The Rosary as a Means to Brotherhood

In 1972 Mother Mary gave us a rosary that can be used by people of all faiths to adore the Divine Mother. She requested that this rosary be a scriptural rosary with Bible verses read between the Hail Mary and other prayers. Mother Mary explained that "Hail Mary" simply means "Hail Ma-Ray" or "Hail Mother Ray," and that the recitation of the Hail Mary praises and evokes the Mother Flame. Mother Mary has asked that we give the rosary daily—either the original scriptural rosary, which takes about an hour, or a shorter rosary of about fifteen minutes, which she released as "A Child's Rosary."

When she gave us this New-Age rosary, she said: "This is the one key. If the student body will take it up, the giving of this rosary daily will enable the flame of the Mother to be anchored in the world and to prevent a great deal of destruction of human life during the days that are ahead."[2]

Mother Mary says: "How beautiful it is to behold faces upturned in holy prayer, in supplication unto the Divine One whom they identify in my person, but who is not confined to my person, but who is all-pervading. For the Divine Mother is the cosmos itself. And it has been my lot to outpicture a fractioned part of it, and in that part was the whole and is the whole. And thus, when devotees of the light pray 'Mary,' so they receive the effulgence of the *Mother Ray*, which is the inner meaning of *Mary*, released from my hands and heart, released from my being.

"Faces upturned in adoration always have the ear of the angels. The angels of the Divine Mother tarry with those who pray the rosary each day or who offer decrees and affirmations as they have been taught in their individual faiths. For the Divine Mother has no one faith, but is universal. Realize, then, that to her all are children of the Most High; all have come forth from the seed of the Father. And by her nourishment, her tender care and regard, she knows that they shall return unto him.

"Therefore, when you pray to the Divine Mother, include in your prayer the supplication for all who know not the meaning of the Mother, for all who have been deprived of the image most holy of the Virgin and Child. . . .

"Until the soul finds the Mother again—the Motherhood of God personified in many heavenly beings and angels—that soul cannot find reunion with the Father. For the child goes to the Father through the Mother. It is the Mother who teaches the child the wisdom of the Father. It is the Mother who draws the children into the heart of nature. It is the Mother, above all, who seals the soul with the patterns of individuality, who draws out by the power of her love the magnetization of the God Flame that is as a kernel of light locked in the heart until the warmth of the Mother's love reaches it as the sun touches the flowers. And so, they begin to germinate even beneath the soil; and so, the soul germinates within man even before the Christ appears on the surface to transform his entire being and world. . . .

"Pray for your children; pray for yourselves; pray for all humanity. Pray that they might also know the Divine Mother.

"How will they come to know that Mother? There is one very important way in which you can assist, and I have come to tell it to you this day. It is that you become the Divine Mother yourself!—that you receive into your arms those who need succor and healing and comfort and compassion. You who are strong men and wise, you too, must become the Mother; you must outpicture her flame. And women of the sacred fire, you who have borne the children of this generation, understand that all people are your children. . . .

"Remember the prayer of Jesus, 'Father, make them one even as we are one.'³ In your hearts and in your consciousness, in your thoughts of one another, will you embrace each other each day as you would the Christ who is cradled and aborning within your heart. For only by this great love for your brother, for your sister, will you come to know the oneness that we share, the oneness of the Mother and of the Christ, the oneness of the Father. . . .

"For in the union of that oneness you find the strength, the overcoming victory and the power that enables you to withstand all of the fiery darts of wickedness and all the temptations of the world."⁴

Mother Mary holds the office of the Cosmic Virgin, not exclusively but inclusively. She includes in her office all those who are one with her, all those who are a part of her devotion to Mother. And she includes you when you say daily:

Hail, Mary, full of grace, the Lord is with thee. Blessed art thou among women and blessed is the fruit of thy womb, Jesus.

Holy Mary, Mother of God, pray for us, sons and daughters of God, now and at the hour of our victory over sin, disease and death.*

---

*Mother Mary has said that Keepers of the Flame ought not to affirm their sinful nature, but rather their rightful inheritance as sons and daughters of God; nor should they dwell upon the hour of death, but rather upon the hour of victory. She therefore asked the Mother of the Flame to teach the Keepers of the Flame to pray for her intercession "now and at the hour of our victory over sin, disease and death," thereby drawing their attention to the hour of victory over all conditions of time and space, which her blessed Son proved in his life and in the hour of his victorious ascension.

In the recitation of the rosary Mother Mary gives us the opportunity to put on the mantle of her consciousness. When you give the rosary, it is like wrapping a single coil of fine filigree gold around the pole of your being. Each day you add another filigree coil, and gradually you come to the place where, almost in spite of yourself, you feel more devout, more holy, more a part of the Mother and much closer to Mary—you can almost feel the shimmering of her robes as she passes by. Day by day, coil upon coil of this filigree gold, you are putting on the mantle of the Mother in preparation for being the World Mother, for being the consciousness of the Cosmic Virgin.

Mother Mary tells us that if an individual is constant in giving the rosary, decrees and prayers, "we may place upon the broad shoulders of that one, broadened by a sense of cosmic responsibility, the weight of the little children suffering in the ghettos and the slums of the world, of the prisoners of war being tortured, of the underground Christians who are giving their lives so that they might be counted among the Christians, of those who are standing up for Truth and for God, for those lifestreams who are prominent in the world in government and religion, in politics, in economics who have not the knowledge of the Law but have the great courage of their convictions. These need the prayers of the saints. These need your love."[5]

And again, she says of the daily giving of the rosary: "Through that action of praise to the Mother ray, you will see how your consciousness will be adorned with the jewels of a Mother's heart; you will see how you will begin to care, to really care about your fellowman. And because you care, you will have the flame of the Holy Spirit that is able to impart at any hour of the day or night that which is the greatest need in your loved ones, in children, in strangers, in all whom you meet.... This is a role, a path and a way that is so important. For as you have been told, the hand that rocks the cradle is the hand that rules the world."[6]

The Office of Mother of the Flame

Down through the ages members of the Great White Brotherhood have come forth to sponsor uplift movements and to assist the lifewaves of earth in every aspect of their evolution. Great artists, inventors, scientists, statesmen and religious leaders have been overshadowed by various members of this spiritual Hierarchy as they formed the avant-garde of achievement in their fields.

In this century, Saint Germain, sponsor of the United States of America and Hierarch of the Aquarian dispensation, stepped forth once again to sponsor an outer activity of the Great White Brotherhood. In the early 1960s he contacted his embodied representative, the Messenger Mark L. Prophet, and founded the Keepers of the Flame Fraternity.[7] The purpose of the fraternity is for the fusion of fiery spirits ascended with souls on earth in a unifying action for and on behalf of the salvation of the children of the light in this age.

Within the Fraternity is the office of Mother of the Flame. This office is held by one who is dedicated to the World Mother and who pledges to serve the sons and daughters of the Flame wherever they are throughout the world. The Mother of the Flame is an honorary title and an office in Hierarchy held successively by unascended feminine devotees appointed by the Great White Brotherhood to nourish, or mother, the flame of life in all mankind.

In 1961 Saint Germain appointed Clara Louise Kieninger as the first Mother of the Flame of the Keepers of the Flame Fraternity. On April 9, 1966 that office was transferred to Elizabeth Clare Prophet, and Clara Louise Kieninger became the Regent Mother of the Flame, an office she continues to hold from the ascended level.

The one who holds the office of Mother of the Flame,

together with all members of the Keepers of the Flame Fraternity, spiritually cares for the world's children. She is responsible for their nurturing, their health, their education and their oneness with God. The Mother of the Flame is also responsible for nurturing all life, bringing all sons and daughters of God to oneness with Jesus Christ and carrying the torch of Liberty so that freedom might reign in every nation.

The Mother of the Flame is the one who holds the Mother Flame on behalf of earth's evolutions, who ministers as the Good Shepherd to the flocks of the nations, the flocks of the world. This office must be held upon earth for the restoration of the feminine ray in connection with the retreat of the God and Goddess Meru at Lake Titicaca, in connection with the raising of the temples of Lemuria and for the restoration of womankind to a role of dignity, leadership, intuition and spiritual attunement for the mothering of the children upon earth.

A Torch of Illumination

On December 31, 1972, Gautama Buddha passed to Elizabeth Clare Prophet, the Mother of the Flame, a torch of illumination and a mission to bring illumination and true culture to the world. Gautama Buddha said: "Some of you may recall one who passed from you some time ago, the first Mother of the Flame, who later became the Regent Mother. Well, I want you to know that tonight at inner levels she is with you. Her name upon earth, Louise Kieninger, will kindle in many of you a response of her great love.

"I want you to understand that her body is no longer gray or crooked in any way. Her form no longer reflects age but only the beauty of her earliest youth and maturity. Upon her face there is a glow of hope and sweetness and love. Her keynote is indeed that which was played to you upon the violin this very evening, 'Calm As the Night.'

"I want you to know that she will be with you until this service shall break up, until you shall leave and depart these doors. She will be with you this night, giving her love and her counsel at inner levels to you, conveying her blessing to you as the first Mother of the Flame. And she shall, ere the night pass, give to the present Mother of the Flame a torch charged with the vital fires from God's heavenly altar and the conveyance of a vast mission to illumine the world's children and produce the blessing of true culture to the age and unto all people everywhere."[8]

This torch of illumination has a tremendous inner momentum of all the Masters who have served illumination's flame, the World Teachers, and from the great retreats of the Brotherhood. The flame of this torch, in its millions of facets, has the pattern of everyone who is devoted to serving the illumination of the planet with the Mother Flame. It is like a giant stained-glass window, with many, many facets. Each facet belongs to someone who has pledged at inner levels to take the torch of divine wisdom and the Divine Mother to a part of the earth, to a section of people, to children or to people of all ages.

Spiritual Culture: The Means of Implementing Brotherhood

True brotherhood must of necessity include a culture* of the Spirit, in order that those who are bound in their common heritage under the Fatherhood of God may have the means to produce in human consciousness the natural order of divine

---

*The inner meaning of *culture* is "cult, or cultivation of light." *Cult* derives from the Latin *cultus,* meaning care, cultivation, culture, adoration; *Ur* (Hebrew 'flame') refers to the center of light or sacred fire. Ur of the Chaldees (Gen. 11:28, 31; 15:7) was an ancient city of light out of which God called Abraham to be the instrument of the incarnation of the seed of Sanat Kumara.

manifestation. Through the cultivation of the light of the Spirit, seeking man can climb the ladder of True Being with the certain knowing that one day he shall be able to express the nobility of his great winged God Self.

Sanat Kumara says that "there must be the renaissance of a spiritual culture, which we term the culture of the New Age, or the culture of the Great White Brotherhood or the culture of the hastening ones. . . .

"Man must understand that he is of the divine nature, a partaker or a communicant of it. If he will understand this, he will be creating a new heaven upon earth, and this is the desire of the Cosmic Ones who desire to create also the image of the hastening one and put that image in the heart and mind of man. This means a fruitful condition will begin to erupt upon the planetary body.

"Why do I use this term *erupt?*

"It is because that which for so long has seemed slow in manifestation will suddenly actually bloom in the heart and mind as though it were what we call a full-blown condition. It will blossom fully very quickly, almost overnight in the consciousness of some, and they will suddenly find themselves possessed of this new awareness and of an eagerness to enter into the fray and assist the planetary body in a way they have never assisted before. They will feel as Saint Paul said he felt long ago. They will very gladly spend themselves and all that they are for humanity and the development of the age and the overcoming of the crisis of the present age. . . . [9]

"Let [men] now understand the need to reinforce the bastions of light so that those bastions may become focuses of greater light everywhere upon the planetary body. And as the focuses expand . . . people will be drawn to them. They will be magnetized to the light, and eventually we will create an entirely new form of ecology upon earth. It will be a manifestation of such beauty as has never been dreamed of by humanity. We will be able to create a new concept in living. Humanity will look forward to it, for they will understand that it represents the care and consideration of the Great Ones....

"We must see to it that throughout the world, throughout the entire planetary body, there is a sense of urgency about the creation of light in the heart that will also reach out into the world with the compassion that is divinely ordained.... The intention of God is to give to humanity the great spiritual heritage that is their portion and thus transmit to them the Reality for which their hearts long."[10]

Spiritual Education

Mother Mary holds within her heart the promise of a truly spiritual education for all of God's children evolving upon this planetary home. Her concern is for the youth of the world that they, too, might come to know the victory that she and Saint Germain helped Jesus to outpicture. In this regard she once said with the fervor that comes from a mother's love:

"The golden lamp of spiritual education is the crying need of the hour. Almost every possible avenue for spiritual education is presently choked by biased secular and sectarian concepts and methods. Dogmatic interpretations are persistently held paramount over brotherhood. The age-old ignorances of men are carefully preserved and made palatable to contemporary man by new disguises in defiance of progress in understanding.

"Amidst this frightful delaying action that deprives men of the kingdom of heaven, the militant and entrenched evils of humanity arise, garbed in robes of social righteousness. These promise the captives of their own lies a form of liberty, while leading them further into the abyss of materialism and those shameful tyrannies whose very tenets are but a parody on true liberty!

"That love for which my son served, and through which he hoped to unite the sons of men, is the strongest possible power to unite the sons and daughters of heaven today in the true understanding that it is spiritual brotherhood, the union of unascended men and women with us [the Ascended Masters] and with God, that will bring forth peace on earth. No mere physical union, be it compounded by the world's most brilliant social scientists, can equal or compare with the blueprint of cosmic glory engraved by the hand of God within each human heart as immortal life in self-sustaining action!

"When the wonders of resurrection in consciousness are experienced by all men, even as they were by my son, Jesus, they too shall say, 'I AM the light of the world,'[11] and so will it be. Each son and daughter of heaven who occupies himself in being about the Father's business is an ally of the Carpenter of Nazareth who will come to equal sonship while showing and teaching all men the most wonderful way through which everyone may achieve world unity and brotherhood."[12]

Opposition to True Education

The Ascended Master Omri-Tas has also spoken of the state of education in the world today: "Educational institutions, while preparing mankind for the rat race, narrow the soul's perception of the Infinite until that precious opening to the universal mind of God is almost closed! And the youth of the world emerge as skeptics, as communists, as fanatics so steeped in their pride that they will no longer consider the humbleness of their parents. They look with disdain upon the hearts that gave them life, whose wisdom is far greater than the science they have supposedly mastered. Well, since the science of this planet is in such a primitive stage, I tell you from our perspective it is no great feat to have mastered that which is known today."[13]

The Ascended Masters are concerned about the youth of the world and the forces that are being hurled against them today. Casimir Poseidon is especially interested in their plight and is determined to help them as much as possible, given their free will.

"You have heard and you have seen that which is being placed upon the youth of the world as a cross, a crucifixion of the soul before the age of maturity. Initiation comes to these little ones, and they are the true and the free and the brave souls who are determined to pass through that dark night of childhood and adolescence into the glory of a victory of a New Day.

"Defend them with a sword of living Truth. Defend them by invocation of the ruby ray. That ray is the intense love of a Mother's heart that cuts as a laser beam across the sordid psychic aspects of the perversions of life upon earth. Invoke the intensity of love to seal these little ones and to dissolve all darkness and error that descends upon their consciousness as a plague of locusts in the land.

"To whom shall they turn? Parents are ignorant of the law of life. Teachers are ignorant and duped.

"Where shall they turn? I ask you to call that they shall turn within and find the angel of the Presence and the guardians of life and a virgin consciousness and the mantle of the Divine Mother to be placed upon them as the swaddling garment of light.

"Let them be taken, then, to etheric temples of light while their bodies sleep. Let them be taken to the etheric schools. Let them be taken to these schools of light where they can unlearn what they are being taught on Terra and have reinforced the blueprint of their fiery destiny. Give your invocations to Mary the Mother. Dedicate your rosary to the plan of life unfolding in the soul. . . .

"In these etheric temples the little children are taught what little children were taught in the Golden-Age civilizations. They are taught the love of life. They are taught to expand the heart, to balance the threefold flame and then to trace a sunbeam from their own heart into the heart of a flower, to commune with elemental life. They are taught to see how love flows, to see the cause of love in the I AM Presence, themselves as the instruments of love and the object of love receiving that vibration, returning that vibration with thanks unto God. And thus, the complete circle of the arc of love is formed.

"And standing in a circle, the children toss the ball of love that they must form by coalescing molecules of the mind, feeling the tangible essence of love received from God, tossed to the next child and the next and the next and returning that love back to the one who first received it from God. And so they learn the cause-and-effect sequences of life.

"Measure for measure, as they sense the vibration of love and work with that energy, they also come to know what it means to misappropriate love. For when they have that fiery sphere of consciousness in hand, because they are yet unascended, because they have their karma and their dharma and their past momentums, they must also deal with the forces of negativity within their own auras. And the compassionate ones, the teachers and the house parents who guard the little cottages where they live, show them how irritation and anxiety and thoughts that are not purely of the Christ will compromise that Flame. They will miss the ball. They will miss the mark. And the ball will be atrophied because they have taken some of its light and put it in another matrix.

"And so, these little children in the temples of the Brotherhood and in the etheric cities are learning daily the lessons that their teachers on earth, through ignorance, have failed to teach them. In the first year of life, the guardian spirits of these little ones teach them to meditate upon the will of God, upon the spoken Word. And they are given instruction through sound and the intoning of the Logos by the angelic hosts. And that which they take into the inner ear, the music of the spheres, they begin to release in the spoken Word. Making sounds, imitating their teachers, they can formulate simple words and tones, vowels and the sound of the name of God.

"Every little child at the etheric plane can say the name *OM*. And every little child understands, without being taught, that this is the vibration of home. And they have the inner knowing because they are taught to see by many methods the white light in the heart and the Flame blazing there. . . .

"And when they return to their physical bodies at the hour of awakening in the morning, they have the impression of the movement and the rhythm of a solar system, a cosmos and the many galaxies and universes within a cosmos, and they sense the rhythm of life. They awaken with joy, with holiness, with a desiring to be free and to strive for perfection on earth. And when they are allowed to frolic in nature at the physical plane, they recall these experiences in the inner retreats, and they have the sense of flow. And by these experiences, the little children have a discrimination and a discernment and they sense the harshness of the world and they know that it is not in keeping with the rhythm of life.

"But by and by, as the children mature, they do not have the full soul faculties to remember these experiences, and if parents and teachers and sisters and brothers are insistent upon impressing upon them the dissonance of the world, they will lose that sensitivity. And the loudness of the rock music as it is played is deafening not only to the outer ear but to the inner ear of the soul, destroying the hearing on the physical as well as the etheric plane, in that the soul's hearing in the etheric octave can no longer be transmitted through faculties to outer awareness....

"The motto that we sought to instill in the children then, we place today in the etheric retreats: 'Learn to love to do well and you shall'—the motto of love inspiring creativity and love inspiring discipline. It is the same yesterday and today and forever, the same impetus to life and overcoming and victory.

"You must love your work, love your sacred labor, love your invocations, love your study to show yourself approved unto the law of life. You must love and love and love and imbue every action with that love. For every action is a matrix, and if it is charged with love, love will leap from heart to heart, from hearth to hearth. Love will leap, and love will be the inspiration to freedom and to joy and to continuing on when all the momentums of darkness, so highly organized as they are today, are as the oncoming of darkness over the land.

"Let this land be returned to Saint Germain. Let it be returned to your own Christ consciousness, to your own souls. Claim the land for the Divine Mother! Claim the land for the victory! Return this civilization to Saint Germain, that the little ones might have the opportunity to fulfill their promises to your hearts."[14]

Thus, we see how different is education in the Golden Age of the etheric octave, and we see glimpses of what education for children could be in a Golden Age here on earth.

The Montessori Method

As we seek the educational systems for a New Age, we find that there have been pioneers in this field who have been inspired by the Ascended Masters to bring forth elements of this vision. This Aquarian revolution in education was begun by Maria Montessori, the famous Italian educator. The following quote summarizes her philosophy:

"If we wish to set about a sane, psychical rebuilding of mankind, we must go back to the child. But in the child, we must not merely see the son, the being in whom our responsibilities are centered. We must consider the child in himself, and not in his relationship to us in dependence.

"We must turn to the child as the Messiah, an inspired being, a regenerator of our race and of society. We must succeed in effacing ourselves until we are filled with this idea, then go to the child as the wise men of the East, loaded with power and with gifts, and led by the star of hope."

This is the idea that every child has the divine spark within, has a Christ Self and a Causal Body, and has within him the knowledge that he needs. Our task is to help the child externalize this knowledge and make it practical in day-to-day life. In essence, we merely unlock the divine potential within the child so he may become all he is meant to be.

Maria Montessori was born in Italy in 1870 and became Italy's first woman medical doctor. When she was serving as a doctor in Rome, she was given an assignment to care for the kindergarten children in the slums of the city. She went into an area where the children were very poor, and there she began to receive her inspiration.

She discovered that children have very different and unique qualities that no one had ever noticed. She found that these qualities, which are resident within childhood, can be liberated and set free in the proper environment with the proper conditions.

And one of the first things she noticed when dealing with children was that they would rather work than play. Children are very industrious, and if you organize their work, you can actually establish patterns that help them to develop, even from the time they are born.

Children have a tremendous love for order—they like to put things back and find things in the same place each day. For example, she taught the children an exercise of washing tables, which is now carried on in Montessori schools throughout the world. It is a complete ritual, because she found that children between the ages of two and seven are great creatures of ritual. They love to do things in order, and the goal of the child is not to get the job done but to do it systematically. She explains that the patterns of order and logic that are developed in the child through physical activity later enhance the child's ability to learn, to concentrate, to study. All these things are what children need if they are going to be taught the Ascended Master way of life.

Montessori found that children have a keen sense of touch, that they learn with their hands more than they even learn with their eyes, and so she designed systems of what she called sensorial development. She used sandpaper cut out in the shape of letters. And by tracing the letters with their fingers, it became etched in the children's memory how the letter is formed. After practicing with the sandpaper for a while, they were then able to use pencil and paper to write the letters and pronounce the sounds the letters make.

She discovered that children like freedom of choice. The classroom is designed to allow each child to select the set of blocks or whatever lesson he is drawn to use at that specific moment—it is a cosmic moment—when his soul is ready to develop around that particular point.

Children ages two-and-a-half through six are all in one classroom so that the younger children can see the more advanced work of the older children and they can learn from their example. A Montessori teacher's role is to direct the child toward the exercises. It is not conducted as a typical classroom where the teacher stands up and the whole class does the same thing at the same time.

In a Montessori classroom you will find little children at their tables preoccupied for great lengths of time, concentrating on their lessons. They have an amazing power of concentration. They learn mathematics with concrete equipment such as beads or blocks designed to teach the association of numerals and quantity. They learn writing and reading, but they do it according to the pattern of their own unique inner development. Children are not rushed or forced to do something that does not come easily and naturally to them. The teacher's role is to encourage independent learning as the child listens to his own inner teacher. Montessori found that the call of the universal child is, "Help me to do it myself."

All of these things were revealed to Maria Montessori by the children themselves. She said that all she did was watch the children, and they taught her the method.

There are a number of foundational principles of the Montessori Method. The first is what she called "the absorbent mind." This is the quality of mind the child has from birth through age six. This is a time when the child can learn effortlessly. He is like a sponge. He pulls in everything from his environment, and he draws in the completeness of it. He does not discriminate by choosing "Yes, I want this; no, I don't want this." Montessori said that he "incarnates" the environment. Once it is incarnated, it is there for life. And that is why birth through age six are the most important years for you to be educating your child and surrounding him with beauty and culture.

She found that the absorbent mind goes through what are called "sensitive periods." Children have sensitive periods for certain activities and certain types of learning, such as language, writing or the development of motor skills. Our task is to discover what these sensitive periods are and to provide the child with the prepared environment and the appropriate lessons that can allow the child to make the greatest use of this window of opportunity. Montessori said that "when a child is in a sensitive period, he is like a living flame, consuming and devouring in his activity all that concerns the special sensitivity of that development, but when the sensitive periods are over, it is as if a flame has gone out." Thus, we see that young children effortlessly learn a new language during the first six years of life, whereas later in life study and hard work would be required.

The next principle of the Montessori Method is the "prepared environment." The furniture and all the implements in the classroom are in proportion to the size of the child. Everything has its own place, and everything is always in that place. This gives the child an ordered environment that will set his mental furniture in order for life. Montessori said that the prerequisite for discipline is precision in the environment.

In the Montessori classroom the teacher shows the children how to do each lesson, and after they have had a presentation, then they can do it by themselves. Children are free to move around, to take lessons off the shelf and to do them as many times as they want, and when they are finished, they put them back. Repetition is common in young children, and you will often see them repeat a lesson many, many times—just for the fun of it. As the children would choose one lesson or another, according to their individual needs and their sensitive periods, Montessori began to see, even in the two-year-olds, the basic beginning of the power of free will.

Discipline is a key element of the method. Montessori said, "Discipline and freedom are so co-related that if there is some lack of discipline, the cause is to be found in some lack of freedom." She said that the dawning of discipline comes through work, through concentration on an exercise that is so interesting that the child chooses to exclude other reactions and other responses. This level of self-discipline that you reach in the classroom is unreachable through direct means of attacking an error in a child or trying to force a child to do something that he does not want to do.

Montessori said: "In our efforts with the child, external acts are the means which stimulate internal development, and they again appear as its manifestation, the two elements being inextricably intertwined. Work develops the child spiritually; but the child with a fuller spiritual development works better, and his improved work delights him, hence he continues to develop spiritually. Discipline is, therefore, not a fact but a path, a path in following which the child grasps the abstract conception of goodness with an exactitude which is fairly scientific.

"But beyond everything else he savours the supreme delights of that spiritual order which is attained indirectly through conquests directed towards determinate ends. In that long preparation, the child experiences joys, spiritual awakenings and pleasures which form his inner treasure-house—the treasure-house in which he is steadily storing up the sweetness and strength which will be the sources of righteousness."[15] If the classroom is orderly, the child internalizes and becomes that order.

The Montessori method is intended to bring out the Christ potential of the child, as the child follows the direction of the inner teacher and selects in the classroom certain equipment and exercises that are appropriate for fulfilling the inner and spiritual needs of the child and bringing forth inner attainment. The combined freedom and order in the Montessori classroom is the true Aquarian-age education.

The Montessori method for children was inspired upon Maria Montessori by Mother Mary. Mary said that this was the method she had devised with Elizabeth for teaching John the Baptist and Jesus when they were children.

Dispensations for Illumination and the Spiritualization of Education

As Lord of the second ray of illumination, Ascended Master Lanto is concerned with the state of education in the world and that education lead to spiritual development and not material knowledge alone. He teaches from the Royal Teton Retreat of the Brotherhood: "Let us point out to the world of men that all the knowledge that mankind have assembled throughout the ages, now currently remaining within the libraries and dossiers of the world, comprises but a pinch of salt compared to the relative knowledge unreleased, unpublished, unknown.

"Let me point out that that which is not now revealed to mankind is so much more than that which has been revealed, that an attitude of total humility on the part of the family of nations and the human family ought to exist throughout the planetary body, that it might become invocative and evocative within man of a search for a Golden-Age renaissance of culture without the limit and restraint of human stops and dams that prevent the flow of the mighty tides of God's energy released as holy knowledge to a world that is waiting indeed for the sunrise of an age of light.

"With the world conditions as they are today, is it not, then, essential that mankind shall have a more full-orbed light of spiritual knowledge that will bring into manifestation the broadening powers of cosmic illumination to put an end to this ignorance that permits them to make peace with feelings within their heart that are hostile? Hostility is within their heart, and prayers are upon their lips. And these are strange bedfellows to the Ascended Masters.

"We call these things to your attention not in order to create a feeling of depression, but to show you the degree to which mankind in this present hour is oppressed by the delusions of the senses and the lack of spiritual practicality.

"Spiritual practicality, then, is the order of the day! And we seek to release tonight the fire of our knowledge into the world of form.

"Therefore, I am asking the Lords of Karma for a special grant this night to spread abroad holy illumination's flame in cooperation with the God and Goddess Meru. I am asking that there be anchored in every university in this land that is receptive to knowledge, especially to knowledge revealed from the higher octaves, a mighty, transcendent, golden flame of illumination that shall pulsate three hundred feet into the atmosphere above each university and shall day after day, hour after hour, radiate Ascended Master light into the forcefield of the students who are attending these universities.

"I am asking that that forcefield be created this night and this day, this hour by God's own light and power of illumination, sustained, then, for all time to come as foci of the sacred fire. I am asking that a fixation be made of these flames, that as the great light blazed forth of old in Atlantis in the Incalithlon, so the great Maxim Light* will now blaze forth as the maximum light of cosmic knowledge within the campuses and forcefields of the universities of the world and also within the divinity and theological schools of the world to create a theological concept based upon divine practicality.

"Mankind has the knowledge of the Law. Mankind has comprehension. They have understanding, but they do not use it. And knowledge unused often passes quickly from the screen of consciousness until it is no longer a thing of beauty and a joy

---

*The Maxim, or Maxin was the spiritual/physical unfed flame that burned on the altar in the great temple of Atlantis, the Incalithlon. It had been placed there by Jesus Christ himself in 15,000 B.C. and it burned until just before the sinking of Atlantis. For a description of this temple and the Maxin Light, see Phylos the Thibetan, *A Dweller on Two Planets* (Borden Publishing Company, 1952).

forever, but rather, it becomes a mere bric-a-brac in the mental attic of their world, cast aside and repudiated by their actions, even as they have cast aside unused garments and things that have outlived their usefulness.

"Now, by the light of cosmic knowledge and by the mind of God infused as the sacred-fire element into the campuses of the universities and thence into the domain of the human heart where it will expand knowledge and make it practical, men will find that they can work together as never before because there is wedded to the spirit of man the alchemical tie that came forth from the heart of God in the beginning and is the chemical marriage that weds Spirit and Matter together to function within the domain of cosmic predictability."[16]

God Meru has announced another dispensation to assist in the education and illumination of mankind: "In the midst of turmoil and unrest, deceit and darkness upon this planet, we come with a scepter of the Christ—point, counterpoint—with a mighty plan for the evolutions of this planet. We come to announce to you this day a program of divine illumination that has been espoused by every member of the Great White Brotherhood, every angel and deva, the mighty Elohim, and even the Cosmic Christ's Messengers from out the heart of the Great Central Sun, for heaven is in one accord this day. And as a result of our council meetings, through great deliberations and a complete and thorough study of the needs of the mankind of this planet, we have concluded that a massive program of illumination, of education in the principles of the Christ is in order.

"And we have the dispensation from the Karmic Board, the mercy that would allow us to take into our temples and retreats at night many lifestreams who otherwise would not merit this dispensation. And by the grace of the flame of the mercy of God, illumination shall come forth, once again, to usher in the Golden Age.

"This proposal, which began in the Darjeeling and Indian councils [of the Great White Brotherhood], in the heart of the Buddha, Lord Himalaya and the Cosmic Christ—this proposal and this program of education shall truly be the torch that shall light the world and bring in the great Golden Age. So great is our hope this day, the hope of the Hierarchy.

"I assure you that your cooperation is needed, that the cooperation of all mankind will be needed, and truly great is the need of the hour for teachers upon the planet. For those who study in the temples and the retreats at night must be awakened by those in form as to the mighty truths that they will be given. But I tell you that this cosmic effort on our part will assist you mightily, and you will find a great receptivity dawning in the consciousness of mankind. And by the power of Archangel Jophiel, you will receive that impetus of illumination's flame upon this planet as you have never known it before in your outer consciousness.

"This is a great day for the forces of freedom, for we are absolutely determined that those who come into the retreats shall be stripped of all human effluvia, of all doubt and fear that would be the impediment whereby they could not take in the illumination of the Christ. And under Jesus and Kuthumi, World Teachers, the Mother Mary and all of the ladies of heaven, there is a program also being instituted for those souls in the younger generations, those who are about to embody— and the little children, they will also be tutored.

"I tell you, the Universities of the Spirit and the schools will be blossoming. They will be full and active every night. And I come to tell you several things that you may do in order to enhance this program. First of all, it is highly important that when souls retire at night that they be prepared to leave their bodies. I ask you to institute a service of decrees in the evening time for these souls that they might be stripped of all astral substance through invocation to Mighty Astrea and the angels of purity and the mighty seraphim from out the Central Sun. I ask you to call to the angels of ministration of Uriel's band and of my band, also, so that those souls who are retiring at night do not take with them in their consciousness the records of the television, the mass media and of the day and of argumentation and all form of human involvement.

"On the other hand, I ask you to step up your calls for illumination to the mankind of this earth. I ask you to call for the wakening of the Christ within them. I ask you to plead—and I say to *plead* with the Holy Christ Selves of all mankind to prepare them for this mighty service of light....

"The hosannas go forth. The angels rejoice—the angel of the Presence of God within every soul—for all know that this can be the turning of the tide, that point where the darkness does become the light.... The darkest hour precedes the dawn. And I, Meru, proclaim to you this day the dawn of victory is at hand!"[17]

The Culture of the Spirit

Brethren in Christ know that if one son of God overcame the world, then every son can do likewise. This is the basic tenet of brotherhood. Education must have as its goal the teaching of children and people of all ages how to become the Christ. All doctrines that challenge this tenet are lies that directly oppose the true brotherhood of man in Christ—in the Christ that is the real identity of every man and the only basis/origination of true and lasting brotherhood.

Through the culture of the Spirit there is developed in men a feeling of teamwork—of striving together as one body—to carve out the destiny of the race that is the common destiny of every man, because all of life is one.

In the culture of the Spirit men learn that a sense of the unity of life and a reverence for every part of life as a part of oneself provide the basis for the Golden-Age civilization.

World Communism: Counterfeit of the Golden-Age Culture

Neither said any of them that ought of the things which he possessed was his own; but they had all things common.

THE ACTS OF THE APOSTLES

World Communism: Counterfeit of the Golden-Age Culture

IN OUR ORIGIN WE HAVE COME FORTH from the Father-Mother God. We have come out of the white-fire core, and we now live in the realms of time and space. We have burst forth as the son, as the daughter, as father, as mother. We have received our identity from the core of the I AM THAT I AM, and now, where do we go? We go to the point of our Christhood, which may take thousands of embodiments for us to realize. How do we attain the personification of the Christ?

If a newborn baby is placed in a dark room and left there, even if the child is fed by electronic or indirect means, the child will not grow, the child will not develop, he will not have a personality, he will be more or less a vegetable. The development of the child comes through interaction with others. In the same way, a Christed being is developed through interaction with other Christed beings.

How do we know the Christ except by example? Thus, we are friends of the Masters, and by this we develop our own

Christ consciousness. It is a process of the imitation of Christ. We read the Ascended Masters' words, we study the lives of the saints, we look to people we know on earth as our contemporaries, and we follow the one who has the greatest light of the Christ.

What is all of this interaction? What is it that makes the individual the Christ?

We call it brotherhood. You cannot have the Christ consciousness without brotherhood, and you cannot have brotherhood without the Christ. The one implies the other. The very definition of Christ is the individualization of the God Flame for the purpose of interaction. There is no purpose for individualization of the God Flame except for interaction with other individualizations of that flame.

"And the light shineth in darkness; and the darkness comprehended it not;" therefore, "the Word was made flesh, and dwelt among us."[1] We did not understand the light of the Christ; therefore, God sent a representative of that Christ, the Son. The Son comes into incarnation and interacts with people: father and mother, the Essene community, the community of Lightbearers. So there is formed a Brotherhood.

Ultimately the Brotherhood is international, interplanetary, intergalactic. It is composed of all Lightbearers, all sons and daughters of God who have ever come forth in all systems of worlds. We are all tied to that Brotherhood as we live its principles.

We find, then, that the nation America was selected by the Great White Brotherhood to be the place where the example of brotherhood would be set forth through the example of individuals fulfilling their Christhood through their own self-initiative. Initiative *is* initiation. The American people take their initiations in the Great White Brotherhood by their own initiative.

For the fullest development of that initiative, Saint Germain planned a limited government with the greatest freedom for the individual and the individual states, and the least control by the federal government. He planned a free-enterprise system with the least interference by federal or local government so that the mastery of time and space and the proving of individual self-worth would be on the shoulders of the individual. As long as this plan of Saint Germain was sustained, there was a platform for initiation, a platform to become the Christ.

However, this plan has been altered during the last century. We find a tremendous turning of the tide to reverse what Saint Germain set forth. We no longer find a free-enterprise system as it was intended to be, but instead, more and more government and a maximum of government controls and a minimum of initiative required on the part of the individual.

This has limited the path of initiation. It has limited the opportunity for the individual to become the Christ and to be accepted as a link in the chain of Hierarchy and as a member of the Great White Brotherhood. We find that today it is more difficult to become the Christ than it was five years ago, ten years ago, fifteen years ago, twenty years ago, and certainly much more difficult than it was when the first settlers came and had to forge a life out of the wilderness. The more rugged the life, the more challenging the environment, the less anyone does for you, the more you are calculated to become the master of your life.

We find now that the government takes from the people what is required for the intelligent development of the Christ consciousness. Not only does the government deprive the people of their money through taxation, but it deprives them of this money through inflation and by making the money valueless. Thus, when people work a labor and a sacred labor of their hands, they do not have returned to them the wealth that they have contributed to the nation. What does this produce?

Lethargy, sloth, indifference, no longer a pulling together of a nation. And it completely destroys development of that Christ potential.

Community: The Initiation of the Holy Spirit

What is the next step of initiation when we have perfected our Christhood, when we have perfected a sacred labor? We have known the joy of the fruits of our labor. We have come into alignment with the fullness of this understanding of God, having come forth from the Father and the Mother and burst forth in the flame of the Christ.

The person who has attained Christhood is now whole. He has shown his individuality by creating his own home, his own family, his own business, his own way of life. He answers to no one. He lives as he pleases. He is free. What happens to such an individual after he has enjoyed this freedom and this individuality for centuries? He is ready for the next initiation—the initiation of the Holy Spirit.

This initiation is the bursting of his consciousness, going back to the white-fire core for repolarization. He comes through the Father and the Mother, and then he manifests the action of the Holy Spirit. The action of the Holy Spirit is community.

The individual has realized self-awareness as the Real Self, the Divine Ego, on the three o'clock line (see fig. 2). This Divine Ego now becomes one among thousands and millions of Divine Egos who have, through that individualization of the God Flame, become so aware of God and the individuality of God that they, by the magnet of that consciousness, have drawn to themselves thousands and millions of people who have that same Self-awareness and who, therefore, are a part of community. The vastness of the individuality of God, in proportion to the individuality of the self, has created a living

FIGURE 2: The Individualization of the God Flame

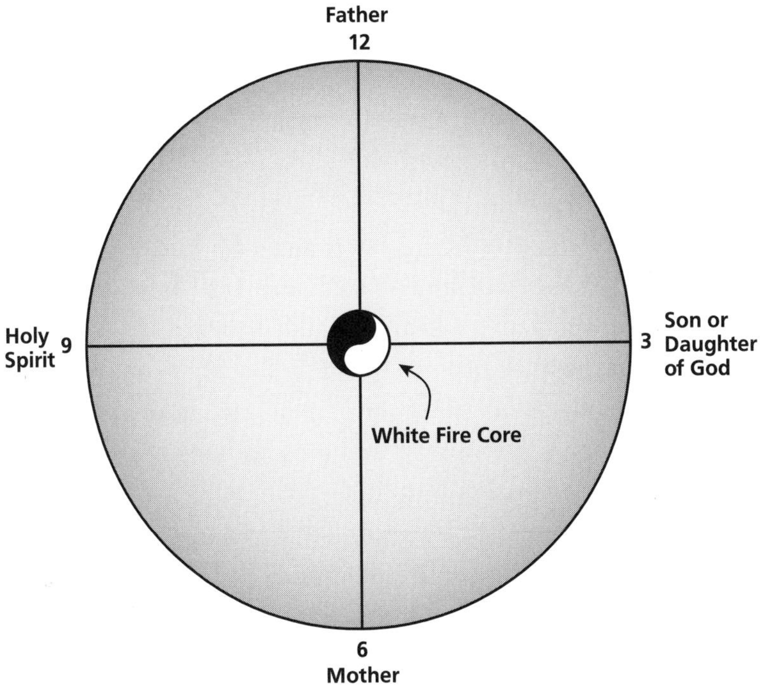

organism of thousands or millions of cells.

In community, each one of us becomes a cell in the body of God. We have such a strong identity in the Christ-potential, such a sense of awareness, that we are as blazing and as flaming as the rising sun at the dawn. How could that sun ever lose itself as that ball of fire, as that energy field? It can merge with a million other suns and separate again and still be that sun. When we have an identity in God, when we have a Divine Ego, we do not any longer fear to lose it. Therefore, we surrender it; and yet we retain it. And we find that our new individuality becomes the community.

All of the laws of freedom that applied in the individualization of the Christ flame now apply at the community level. But instead of one individual determining the course of events, being the breadwinner, having a business, and so forth, we may have a hundred or a thousand individuals who have decided that they understand each other as one being, as one body of God, as one community. And they realize that if they combine their sonship, combine their flames, that they will have that much more power to do and fulfill the purposes that they aspire to fulfill.

The fulfilling of these purposes can no longer be accomplished by the individual alone. Because his Christ consciousness has given him such an expanded awareness of earth's evolutions, he must become the Holy Spirit. He must become a part of perhaps first the twelve, then one hundred, then five hundred, then one thousand and then millions of souls united in one common goal.

Christ and his apostles formed a community. They were also the foundation of a brotherhood, and that brotherhood has come to be known as Christianity. Within Christianity there is an overall community of agreement—we are all Christians— and within that overall agreement, there are individual units who are tighter-knit communities because of their common beliefs.

For the ultimate fulfillment of community, the Ascended Masters have devised an entirely different economic system. This is the pattern of the Community of the Holy Spirit, which we see illustrated in the early Christian Church: "And all that believed were together, and had all things common; and sold their possessions and goods, and parted them to all men, as every man had need."[2] This path of the Community of the Holy Spirit has been perverted in this age by the abuses of Communism. Community without the attainment of the Christ has become communalism, or Communism.

When you force community upon individuals who do not have first the attainment of the Christ consciousness and the tie to the Great White Brotherhood, you have totalitarian states.

You have the forced redistribution of wealth. You force people to do work to which their individual genius is not suited.

This becomes the stripping of the individual of his Christ-identity, of what he has developed of individual genius, before that Christ-identity is complete. It is stripping the nations of their individual identity, their group karma and their group dharma. It is forcing a Community of the Holy Spirit, first as the Union of Soviet Socialist Republics, and then forcing the entire world to come into this community of World Communism before the individuals of that world have attained to the Christ consciousness. Skipping the step of initiation, it becomes the total perversion of the Holy Spirit.

The Philosophy of Communism

Those who would implement the plan of God for the true brotherhood of man should recognize that the philosophy of World Communism is a counterfeit of the Golden-Age culture.

Communism in its modern form is based on dialectical materialism, which is a doctrine based on Karl Marx's adaptation of the Hegelian dialectic to the study of history. Saint Germain explains the fundamental errors in Marx's philosophy:

"Some of you are aware that the study of the relationship of opposites in the planes of relativity is reflected in the dialectic of the nineteenth-century German philosopher Georg Hegel, who theorized that man's thought process and all historical change result from the interplay of three elements: thesis, antithesis and synthesis. According to this observer of life's forces, every thesis generates its opposite, or antithesis, and the interaction of the two produces a synthesis that transcends both. The emerging synthesis in turn becomes a new thesis, and the entire process is repeated again and again.

"Thus, in the Hegelian dialectic all progress is brought

about through the inevitable conflict of opposing forces—a principle Karl Marx turned upside down in his 'dialectical materialism,' wherein he replaced Hegel's idealism with economic materialism. Whereas Hegel supported the value of the state and saw in the dialectical process the unfoldment of spiritual principle, Marx branded the state a mechanism of exploitation and claimed that all progress arises from conflicts involving the economic means of production.

"You who understand the premise of the Ascended Masters' teachings to be the Law of the One do not always take into account this law of relativity governing relative good and evil, perceived by psychologists, scientists and the worldly philosophers. Moreover, in the world of maya, where good and evil are always 'relatively' in opposition, we must also reckon with the negative misqualification of the Absolutes of Power, Wisdom and Love upon which we have been discoursing. Therefore we would touch upon both the human and the divine equations.

"The Law of the One, based on the unity of Being, also functions within the framework of human reason and human events and when it comes full circle in the individual's experience, supports Truth and exposes error.

"But in the human 'two-eyed' perception of the world acquired after the departure from the Edenic self-knowledge in and as the One—when the worldview of man and woman was no longer single in the immaculate All-Seeing Eye of God but the same as that of the band of seducing fallen angels called serpents—there were unalterably two sides to every human equation, with the pendulum swing hot/cold, left/right, always just waiting to happen.

"Not so in the divine equation. Here the true Divine Polarity of Alpha and Omega, the plus/minus of the Godhead, and of each member of the Trinity are the Masculine/Feminine counterparts of Being. These are complementary, not opposing, always fulfilling the Law of the One as the Divine Whole. But in the human condition, just as there is a positive pole, so there is a negative pole to a given situation. These are opposing forces, rivalrous in nature and mutually destructive. For example, if the thesis be human love, its antithesis will be some form of love's polar opposite—human hatred, fear, suspicion or even mild dislike. Their synthesis will be a watered-down version of both with no commitment either to one or the other.

"This is the lukewarm state of mediocrity that Jesus spurned when he said, 'Because thou art lukewarm, and neither cold nor hot, I will spue thee out of my mouth.'[3] And this is precisely why the economic evolution of mankind according to Marx and Lenin can never lead to the divine conclusion: self-transcendence according to the law of love, the Law of the One, which self-contains the true Trinity—power, wisdom and love—as the triad of every man and woman's being."[4]

Marx proposed that the study of man could be reduced to purely material considerations and that economic systems were the primary determinant in relationships between men. Marx adapted the dialectic of Hegel in his statement that "the history of all hitherto existing society is the history of class struggles,"[5] and his concept that all social order founded on class division has within it the seeds of its own destruction until a classless society emerges. Revolution becomes a tool to this end, if necessary.

With the classless society as the absolute goal, history is said to be leading civilization to an inevitable structure where all personal, educational, social and environmental differences are leveled to a predetermined state of so-called equality. Such a state would bring to a halt the operation of the law of karma. Thus, for all intents and purposes, it would preclude the possibility of individuals and nations making spiritual progress, for karma is indeed the great teacher of mankind.

Communism interferes with man's freedom to choose his way of life, to mold his destiny or to become what God intends him to be. His only choice is to make himself an instrument of the state. He must tear down his individuality and then rebuild it according to the image of the state. His destiny is to serve and glorify the state.

The Communist state, as the supreme master of its citizens, precludes the possibility of the individual attaining self-mastery, unless he is an extraordinarily strong spirit. For it destroys his will, his creativity, his self-respect—and above all, his opportunity to take his place in the hierarchical scheme to fill his position in the mandala of the Golden-Age culture.

Communist doctrine makes no provision for man to evolve spiritually while he builds the foundations for the Golden Age. And most important of all, it denies his opportunity to work out his karma within the framework of an economy that allows him to rise according to his own effort.

Unless man is free to work out his salvation (his karma) with pain and suffering,[6] if necessary, there can be no real brotherhood. For brotherhood is based on the soul's realization that "yes, I am my brother's keeper—not because the state forces me to be, but because even as the Father is in me, so am I in every son of God." Communism destroys the basic union of the soul between God and man, and between man and man. Thus, it cannot bring about true brotherhood under the Fatherhood of God.

Christian Brotherhood: Antidote to Communism

The Master Morya comments: "It was due to the lack of Christian brotherhood in action that Communism was spawned upon the world scene. It will be the institution of a genuine and penetrating faith that crosses the lines of religious idealism, dogma, creed and class distinction that will prove to be the universally needed solvent to vitalize and magnify the expansion of world brotherhood."[7]

Alexander Gaylord and Chananda, speaking of a future "Community of the Spirit" where individual dignity will be upheld by the light of its own divinity, foretell that the time will come when "Communistic and Socialistic doctrines will be stripped of their false veneer and revealed to be—as, in reality, they are—methods that were evolved humanly as the result of the intellectual rebellion on the part of their founders against their own personal karma.

"The spiritual community of the enlightened will expound the real democracy of the new republic, wherein the nobility of life in its God-intended expression is its own acknowledged reward. No one will expect to be given honors or rights he does not deserve; neither will anyone expect to deny to others their just opportunity to expand their understanding, test their spirituality or pursue life, liberty and true happiness to the fullest."[8]

The Divine Ideal of Community

The Great Divine Director tells us: "In the community there is enshrined the worth of the individual as the individual is able to integrate consciousness with others who serve in the wave, the ongoing wave, of life. Community is part of the training given in the retreats of the great Masters; for there comes a time on the Path when each initiate is required to prove that he can be effective not only alone with his God, but all-one with fellow servants on the Path.

"Thus in community, in *com*ing into *unity*, sons and daughters of God learn of shortcomings, of failures; and they unite their strengths to overcome their common weakness.

Thus, united in the Flame, they are able to tackle the problems that beset each member of the group and each cell. You see, then, that a retreat experience and an experience in community is often that link to Hierarchy that must be had ere the individual initiate can rise to a greater level of awareness.

"We come then to the subject of community as the repository of individual worth and individual genius. The flame that is enshrined in the community is the Flame of the Holy Spirit....

"The Holy Spirit, the eternal Comforter, is an aspect of the personality of God with the impersonality of the Flame. Some of you have felt the presence of that impersonal, very personal Presence; and you have come to understand how that fire, that specific frequency of light, adorns individual creativity, sparks individual genius and makes the supreme presence in the community of the sacred labor the very keystone in the arch of true building.

"The sacred labor is the ritual of each lifestream by gift, by grace, by talent bestowed from the heart of God. Each member of the community is able to pursue the ritual of life, of self-mastery, of mastery of time and space, all the while cooperating with and supporting the sacred labor of each one. And each one's labor, each one's meditation upon service as a holy thing, a holy act, comprises a thread of gold. And thus, the fabric of community is woven as one garment, as the seamless garment of the Lord's body and of the mandala that all members of the spiritual community focus through their individual heart flames.

"In this age, Hierarchy seeks to externalize a veritable community in the physical octave through Keepers of the Flame and other Lightbearers upon the planet. We seek to externalize in the plane of Mater that which already exists as fact in the plane of Spirit. This age is chosen because it is the Age of Aquarius, the age of divine ritual; and it is through ritual as the sacred labor that mankind will fulfill the epitome of a new-age civilization and of a transition from the old order to the new order."[9]

The Lady Master Meta, who has long served on the fifth ray of science and healing, points out that "the advent of new scientific miracles was intended to provide a very marvelous life for mankind, relatively free from drudgery, so that he might pursue the things of the Spirit. The world has been caught, instead, in a net of delusory violence and ceaseless class struggle. Communism vies with capitalism, and the worst elements of both engage large masses of humanity and vast energy fields in the competitive struggle. The churches, which were intended to be instruments of deliverance for mankind, are more engaged in the struggle with one another than they are in the training of mankind for the business of life.

"The Lord Christ, who taught long ago in the tradition of Melchizedek, priest of Salem, brought forth a reiteration of Golden-Age law: 'As ye would that men should do to you, do ye also to them likewise.'[10] Modern man has inverted this law, making it to read, 'Outsmart your brother before he outsmarts you.'

"The awesome responsibility of the spiritual devotee is to do the good that he would have done unto him, unto all, even to those who despitefully use him.[11] The power of each godly example, of each man who will take his stand for love, pure and undefiled, is thereby set into motion in society; and this is the little leaven that leaveneth the whole lump.[12] The healing elements of golden acts not only purify the individual mind and being, unfolding clearly a wonderful life for those who so dedicate themselves, but also they uphold the power of good example for all men to follow."[13]

The Golden-Rule Ethic: Foundation for Golden-Age Culture

Truly, the Golden-Rule ethic is sufficient for a Golden-Age culture. When men submit themselves willingly to the Laws of

God, they will no longer be threatened by a superstate that would compel them to come under the dominion of man-made laws. God-control and Christ-dominion preclude the possibility of nations or individuals dominating one another's destiny.

Lord Lanto explains the necessary requirements for the Golden Age: "The Golden Age can manifest, beloved ones, only when the Golden Rule is universally lived. I am certain that neither your efforts nor ours are in vain. Although it has well been said of the kingdom, 'few there be that find it,'[14] it has also been prophesied correctly that God shall wipe away all tears from human eyes and that all shall one day know the Lord and manifest the God-ordained perfection of the higher spheres.[15] Thus, the kingdom of heaven in the vision of the Apocalypse is to be ultimately set up upon earth, and the permanent Golden Age, the reign without end, shall begin and forever continue for this planet and all of her evolutions.

"Only then can the Hierarchy safely turn its attention elsewhere to assist other systems of worlds where the development is likewise evolutionary. For among the Father's 'many mansions,'[16] the earth is but a cosmic speck of dust in a sea of spacial light and transcendent suns."[17]

Brotherhood as a Spiritual Ideal

Master Morya outlines the problem of division in the world community and how it can be overcome: "Problems facing the world community are identical to those that challenge city and state governments, although chauvinism and separatism are magnified and more complicated in the larger community. The world scene is also blighted by areas of superstition and ignorance, whose taboos hinder progress and impede the establishment of wells of understanding. It is permissible to launch a spiritual attack against impersonal, entrenched divisions through the effort of united prayer in order to exalt once again the original spirit of Christian brotherhood. It is for this service that we look to the chelas of the Great White Brotherhood. . . .

"Whatever the attitudes that have divided men in the past, these will continue to divide them until a higher state of attunement with God, Self and man is reached. As a caterpillar sheds its cocoon, so must men leave behind outgrown encumbrances and divisive factors. It is not sufficient for a few good men to champion the causes of brotherhood, albeit heaven knows their energies are needed! The garlands of the spiritual principle of brotherhood must be cherished by all nations, by all people and actively honored by men of every organized religion.

"Most men presently in embodiment have been victims, in either the present or the past, of some degree of personal sin or error of omission or commission. Honest men find it difficult to speak out as strongly as they might against the error of those who are performing the same mistakes they themselves have made in the past. Dishonest men take full advantage of the lofty post of judge in order to sit in the seat of the scornful while lifting themselves by unjust human imagination to a false position that will one day be righted by the tipping of the Karmic Scales into balance.

"The truly wise leave all judgment to God and pursue brotherhood as a spiritual ideal, ever holding the concept of discipleship and the ascension into perfection, while keeping the door to true brotherhood open. Such as these compassionately recognize all men as climbing step-by-step the rungs of the ladder of attainment, and although they may dwell temporarily upon the different heights to which they have attained, the wise foretell the day of their ultimate victory above the stages and steps of all human concepts and hold for their brother-pilgrims the immaculate concept of perfect Christ-discrimination."[18]

The Problem of Economic Inequality and the Principle of the Abundant Life

Lord Maitreya, our Cosmic Christ and Planetary Buddha, explains the problem of economic inequality from the Ascended Masters' viewpoint: "The establishment of a unity of world religions through a synthesis of truth is far off and will remain so unless humanity approach the grace of God with both an openness of heart and an inner understanding of the principles of brotherhood. Most men draw nigh to the principle of brotherly love with their lips, but their heart-of-action is far from being manifest. With minds full of condemnation and seething with emotion against one another, they think to approach the throne of grace.

"We are concerned, therefore, with dispelling confusion by our light drawn from the councils, both Eastern and Western, of the Great White Brotherhood and with giving forth those spiritual instructions that will create a clarity of vision for all. Therefore, we submit herewith our concepts concerning a current problem that is being blown up out of all proportion to reality in order to spread abroad violence and confusion.

"I refer to the principle of the abundant life and to the problem, so-called, of economic inequality. There is a constant din that can be heard in the world, a clamor from those who have not against those who have. An interesting sidelight is that the babel of voices for the 'have-nots' and against the 'haves' is being joined by many among the upper class who, in effect, are begging their own destruction.

"Let me hasten to say that all wealth belongs to God, that the earth is his, and that he has asked man to take dominion over it and to share in the practical proof of the principle of the abundant life. This life is, was and always will be for all. Man does not need to create equality; God has already created it. We call it the equality of opportunity. Those who are willing to make application sincerely, to study to show themselves approved unto God[19] and to the wise men of the world are always able to draw forth supply even to the point of being able to give generously to others.

"The philosophies of Communism and of the supremacy of the state may thrive on what we will call a false humility, the wearing of garments of protest and the shunning of more refined aspects of living. This is the sacrifice of individual self-mastery to the lowest common denominator of the group karma. Those who promote these attitudes either do not understand, or they are unwilling to accept, the reality that man's spiritual and real progress does not come from outward sources but from his own reality and the sense of beauty that he holds within. There is no sin in the individual accumulation of wealth or in the manifestation of wealth, for this is a divine privilege that is given to all. All may live in fine houses, wear fine clothing and share in the beauty that creative discipline within an abundant culture can bring forth.

"There is never any need whatsoever for humanity to turn against one another, as did Cain against Abel, in the fear that they have not or will not receive an equal share of the Father's love. All activities of criticism and condemnation are destructive, and they lead inevitably toward a violent climax. The way to real peace in the world for every nation, both at home and abroad, is to amplify the concept of the abundant life.

"Peace is best preserved by adhering to the principles of freedom; for freedom is also tolerant of the thoughts and ideals of others, even when those thoughts and ideals are based on an incomplete understanding of the Laws of God. But the exercise of tolerance does not forego for any man his right to attempt—not by argument, but by an objective presentation of fact—the correction of his brother's error.

"The members of the Great White Brotherhood are concerned that the principle of harmony be found in operation upon earth. In order to further that end midst the struggles of the masses for economic equality, we would point out that for generations there have been those who have, in effect, taken the vow of poverty and who have eschewed the accumulation of wealth. For them, poverty itself has become a virtue; on the other hand, many follow the way of poverty simply because they are unwilling to make the effort to do a great work in the world. They lack either the capacity or the will to create for themselves an abundant life. Both should understand that the laws of love are best practiced and mastered from within.

"We do not condemn those who wish to live in poverty or those who wish to remain in humble surroundings; rather we would point out that it is *nonattachment* that the Law requires of the individual no matter what his station in life—and this means nonattachment to persons, places, conditions and things. Man can be just as attached to his state of poverty as he can be attached to things, and very often we find that poverty becomes a soap box from which those who have not criticize those who have.

"Those who follow in the steps of the Brotherhood see all things as belonging to God, and they see themselves as stewards of his grace. They have, then, no inhibitions as to the earning of large sums of money and the using of that money for their fellowmen. They recognize that creativity can harness the secrets of the universe for the good of all. And they seldom criticize those who do not have an abundance of this world's goods—those who espouse poverty or the kind of life that on the surface seems to be based on a philosophy of nonattachment.

"Those who would rise politically in the world often capitalize on the weaknesses of humanity in order to achieve their ends; their method is to set one segment of society against another by using both secular and religious issues to divide and conquer the minds of men whose hearts are, in reality, one. This tactic is often the root and only cause of the underlying social problems that confront individuals and nations today.

"True faith in God is faith in the abundant life. It should be of no concern to you what your neighbor is able to gain of this world's goods or even how he employs his gain so long as it is done honestly. People should rejoice in the abundance of others as they would rejoice in their own abundance; and they should see that when men are able to produce abundantly and to remain in a calm state of good will to all, they not only enjoy life, but also they are able to support institutions and activities that will sustain and preserve God's beauty on behalf of all men.

"The ugliness of the world manifests through man's criticism of man.... It can only degrade, by the downward spiral, the one who engages his energies in the practice of criticism.

"The principle of the abundant life is the principle of the Great White Brotherhood that keeps the soul open to God from the top and that enables the flow of Reality to beam constantly into the chalice of the individual lifestream. As the Reality of his True Self becomes more real, he sees in the natural order of manifestation, the inward perfection of the Edenic state that existed before the fall of his consciousness into the density of an ego-centered existence.

"It is easy, precious ones of the light, to criticize; but it is even easier to hold the principle of the abundant life in your consciousness. It is easier to enhance the meaning of life for others than it is to rob them of their virtue by a constant damning (con-demn-a-tion) of their attitudes and the spiritual processes they have evolved. Be it so that they are surrounded with error—the purpose of life in the evolutionary stream is the shedding of error and the mastering of perfection. If you force the issue, you may break the slender thread that is leading them on to the very truths you would have them accept in your time instead of in God's time. Man did not come into manifestation in order to lose his life, but he came to gain all of God-good.

"We who are concerned with the initiation of each individual are also concerned with the initiation of society. The total identity of a free society is inextricably interwoven with the thoughts and ideals of its people. A free society can rise no higher than the thinking of its best leaders, and these are constantly being assaulted by the negative concepts of forces that attempt to tear down all that serves the nobility of the Christ in the individual and in society. The sense of struggle must be shed, and the windows of life must be opened wide that the fresh, clean air of the Christ consciousness may renovate the life process.

"We have seen enough of despair, engendered by those whose own frustrated egos lead them into forms of exhibitionism that are calculated to raise their personalities into prominence. We are concerned only with the raising of divine ideas into prominence and with the exaltation of divine ideas in the minds and hearts of men, for these are the ideas that will make men free. Hold on, then, with the very teeth of your being to the principle of the abundant life. Develop God's consciousness of the abundant life for yourself. Expand it until you can clearly see that it is not the Father's will that man should perish or live in limitation or lack.

"Whether the seeker is a divine poverello as Saint Francis of old or a businessman of worldly fame and means, he should seek the correct use of his stewardship,[20] and above all, he must be ready to accept the possibility that his personal philosophy, his developed concepts and his opinions of long standing may not necessarily be correct. Be willing to examine Truth, and beware of the trends spread abroad through the media designed to divide and to confuse the world. 'Pure religion undefiled before God and the Father' has been defined as the visiting of the widows and the orphans and the keeping of oneself unspotted from the world.[21]

"In the sense of the abundant life, let good works abound; and let these include the purification of the consciousness so that the corrosions of the world, both secular and religious, do not disturb the beautiful fruit from the Tree of Life that God seeks to nourish in every soul.

"How great he is, and how great man can be! How abundant and delightful are his hopes and plans for all of humanity. Let men joyously receive his concept of the abundant life for all."[22]

El Morya gives the Ascended Master antidote to Communism and a formula for the abundant life. He says: "Most problems are centered in the marketplace of life's basic necessities. Therefore, give knowledge, bread and opportunity to all, and strengthen, thereby, the most natural deterrents to war and Communism. Reduced to its simplest expression, the formula for world goodwill and happiness is this: Feed the hungry, teach the ignorant and love the people of the whole world as yourself. Sponsor this unity of goodwill, and the earth will prosper."[23]

The Solution to the Economy and the Labor Crisis on Earth: The Violet Flame

Omri-Tas shows us that the divine solution to labor problems in our economy lies in the education of the heart and an understanding of the violet flame: "From the perspective of the Ascended Masters, knowing what the release of the violet flame can do for a single life and an entire planetary lifewave, we realize that it is the education of the heart itself that is wanting. If each lifestream had this education from birth, it would enable that one to so easily draw down the violet flame from the I AM Presence and then watch the violet flame and the elementals and the violet-flame angels perform those tasks that mankind consider drudgery.

"Have you thought about the fact that there is a labor crisis on planet Earth? Have you thought about the fact that many people are educated far above the jobs they are required to take? Have you considered the fact that many nations are so educated that they must import workers from other nations to perform the necessary menial tasks? And in many cases these workers are of an order and an evolution such as those who migrated to Atlantis in the last days. They are laggard lifewaves who ultimately tipped the karmic balance against the Light-bearers and were a major factor in the sinking of that continent.

"When a single people and a karmic group cannot provide for all of the necessities of life and do not determine to be self-sufficient, and when they begin intermingling with those evolutions that have a separate karma and dharma and a separate duty, or reason for being, to fulfill . . . this commingling of the races causes a breaking down of their perception of the separate dharma, or duty, that is to be fulfilled. And this commingling is also an interference with each of these groups balancing their separate karma. . . .

"I direct your attention to this understanding, that through the balanced action of the seven rays, the evolutions of earth can move forward. The violet flame is the necessary and key ingredient to the problem of labor and to the sanctification of that labor on planet Earth.

"We see the problems in the economy. We see those who have performed services that are no longer in demand lose their jobs and means of livelihood because technology is advancing beyond their levels of attainment, including the development of the heart. The heart, therefore, is the seat of the balanced expression of the Trinity ennobling and therefore 'enabling' each lifestream to fulfill his reason for being—'heart, head and hand'; and the heart chakra is the point for the issue of (that is, the release of) the violet flame.

"The violet-flame angels and the elementals who serve with them have a great and intense desire in this hour to make known to you how important it is that this violet flame and the understanding thereof be spread abroad in the earth so that once again, by the education of the heart and by the sons and daughters of God being engaged in those activities that they ought to be engaged in, the true complementary office of angels and elementals might, therefore, be performed. . . .

"Due to the absence of the violet flame, we see imbalance in nature. And due to this imbalance in nature not checked by the violet flame, you see the imbalance in the psyche of the people. You see mounting conditions of psychological problems, divisions within the self, within the four lower bodies. You see moodiness, moroseness and the 'split personality,' as you say. And then you see the body affected—for inasmuch as the environment is not balanced by the violet flame through the threefold flame of the heart, there is the resulting imbalance in the chemistry of the body.

"Some have wondered, 'What is the use of the violet flame in a Golden Age or a place of perfection?' The violet flame establishes and reestablishes the rhythm of life. It is like the oil in the gears of modern civilization. It is a very special quality of the Holy Spirit that all have need of daily, just as you need the sun and the many frequencies of the stars and the earth currents and the air and the water, and the power of integration with all of these.

"We say, therefore, that our assistance to Gautama Buddha, to the mighty Elohim and the Archangels does come because we have understood that the saving grace of all planetary homes and of every lifestream is this missing link of the seventh ray. The absence of the violet flame is a missing link in the chain of earth's evolution. And so you can see how evolution, as it were, is out of whack with the lunging forward of some talents and skills while other parts of the human being remain almost at the primitive state; for primitive states of anger and the passions in the unconscious—of hatred, rivalry and base instincts of self-preservation—have not been submitted by free will to the transmutative fires of the violet flame. . . .

"When you espouse the life of holiness and recognize that a planet and a people depend on the nourishment of holiness, you will discover the true priorities of your calling in God. And you will also discover a wellspring from on high that allows you to accomplish more in less time and therefore, to indeed fulfill your physical responsibilities while remaining, as it were, a 'closet priest' of the sacred fire, a 'closet priestess' of the violet flame. It is not necessary to walk about in robes of the Ancient of Days, but it is indeed necessary and possible for you to keep the Flame. . . .

"It all boils down to common sense and to thinking in logical order and to arranging your life systematically. Those who are the achievers have learned to do this, and those who achieve not and become a weight moving in the opposite direction of our stated purposes are those who have never quite determined to challenge their own confusion and the rebellion that is behind the confusion. For confusion is a rebellion against the order of God and ultimately, against God as Mother, who must order the entire Matter cosmos.

"Now, an absence of ordering your day may be a factor in your not invoking the violet flame, even as time seems to escape those who have not taken the opportunity to master its cycles. And space itself becomes cluttered in the homes of those who have not yet determined to master the laws of space, acknowledging that the mastery of space is the mastery of the Buddha even as the mastery of time is the mastery of the Mother....

"Some of you know that you, personally, are doing the work of two or five or ten people. You do it gladly and joyfully, for you recognize the urgency of the hour. Others, however, I am sorry to say, do not fulfill even the requirements of one life for their failure to intensify the application of their hearts' love to the work at hand. And still others, by their absence of resolution of their psychology, cannot think of anything to do, cannot think of what their job should be, their calling, their profession or where they should direct their attention.

"This is amazing to us when we see a planet in such suffering and so many people in need. One has but to turn around, and one will see five mouths to feed and this mess to clean up and that task to be accomplished. And thus, you see that the inability to recognize the need of the hour and to take care of it is an absence of true perception, which in turn is an absence of the true integration of the chakras with the heart flame. And this comes back to the problem of the imbalanced threefold flame and the lack of the violet flame. Practicality is always the sure sign of a balanced threefold flame and a developed heart chakra. And without these, there is no momentum to sustain the violet flame.

"The violet flame tunes the seat-of-the-soul chakra. And at that point of the seat of the soul, one knows who I AM, where I have come from, where I am going, and what is the work that is assigned to me in this life....

"There *is* a divine plan. And the task that is yours and yours alone is difficult. It *must* be difficult. It is given to you in order that you may transcend your last life or the activities of a decade ago. You are here in embodiment to pursue the calling of excellence. You *must* overcome. It is the law of cosmos. This is spiritual evolution. Your soul must increase in magnitude, putting on greater light and wisdom.

"You will not get this God Self-mastery by performing the task you have done for the past ten embodiments, which is easy, requires no thought, no effort. You can cease to think, cease to create and almost cease to be while you continue to perform that same task over and over again, and you say to yourself: 'I'm earning enough money to support my family. Everything's OK in my life. Here I am. I don't have to worry about war. I don't have to worry about planetary conditions. Those are not my problem. I am here safe in my little house and I can do what I will do and I can enjoy myself and have good times with my friends and my children.'

"You see, the effort that must be expended to perform the mission is the same effort that must be expended to win the next level of initiation. . . .

"There is a time for self-correction, which has nothing to do with self-condemnation! A mistake begets a joyous desire for excellence, for self-overcoming, for reaching the star, for being like El Morya. It is not a question of guilt. It is not a question of sin. It is not a question of self-flagellation. It is a realization of limitation: 'I will conquer! I see this. I will cut through it. I will put it behind me.'"[24]

The Twelve Tribes of Israel

But go rather to the lost sheep
of the house of Israel.

JESUS

The Twelve Tribes
of Israel

T HE STORY OF THE TWELVE TRIBES OF
Israel is usually thought to have
begun with Abraham, the progenitor and first patriarch of the
Hebrew people. But, in reality, their record on earth begins
much earlier, with the coming of Sanat Kumara, the Ancient of
Days.[1] He came on a rescue mission at the time that was the
lowest and darkest moment in earth's history.

A Cosmic History

The first three root races had lived on Lemuria in a time
when all that was ever known on earth were Golden Ages and
there was not a descent through disobedience to the Laws of
God. This disobedience took place during the epoch of the
fourth root race.

The Great Rebellion of Lucifer and his angels had begun to
infect several planetary worlds. Planet Earth was also infected,
and thousands of years ago, in the mists of Lemuria, there

occurred the Fall of man—the desecration of the flames of Father and Mother, the misuses of the sacred fire.

In the midst of all of this, the great teacher Lord Maitreya came to establish his mystery school, recorded in Genesis as the Garden of Eden; and this is where the Biblical account of the history of man begins. Maitreya called on a son and a daughter of God to enter this mystery school to redeem and atone for the sins of mankind—and we can see that sin was already present on earth in the very presence of the Serpent himself.

That opportunity for redemption was failed by that son and daughter of God. Through disobedience to God's laws and the direction of the Guru, they were expelled from the mystery school. Because of the wickedness of mankind and their failure at the opportunity for redemption, Lord Maitreya told them that they would have to wait thousands of years for another opportunity and that the opportunity would come through the incarnation of the Word in the beloved Son, the Christ.

The opportunity for redemption in the Garden of Eden was given long after darkness had appeared on the land. Following this episode, there was the sinking of the continent of Lemuria and the sinking of the continent of Atlantis, which is recorded in the Bible as the Flood.

The Coming of Sanat Kumara

Even prior to these events recorded in the Bible, there was that point following the Fall of man when the earth was in her darkest hour. The Cosmic Council that governs the destiny of the earth decreed the dissolution of the planet and her evolutions because every single person on earth had forgotten the Source and the threefold flame.

At that time, Sanat Kumara, the hierarch of Venus, came before the Cosmic Council and said, "I will volunteer to be the saviour of the earth. I will volunteer to keep the flame of the earth until some among mankind awaken to the knowledge of the Law." Sanat Kumara was granted the opportunity to come to earth to keep the flame.

When the Lightbearers of Venus, Mercury and other planetary homes heard that he was volunteering to stand for the evolutions of earth, they volunteered to go with him and were accepted. And thus, when Sanat Kumara came to earth, there was a retinue of Lightbearers who came with him to establish Shamballa, his retreat on the White Island in the Gobi Sea (which is now the Gobi Desert in China).

The retreat of Sanat Kumara became the permanent focus of the light of the threefold flame of Father, Son and Holy Spirit, which mankind of earth had lost through their animalism and degradation. The establishment of that focus was for the purpose of keeping that Flame and reigniting the Flame in the hearts of the people.

The Incarnation of the Lightbearers

Those who came with Sanat Kumara were to embody according to a prearranged destiny among the nations of the earth. Their mission was to be the Lightbearers who would teach mankind the way of the Trinity, the way of the threefold flame, the way of the sacred fire, and remind them of their origin. They would come, then, to the East and to the West, and they would come to teach mankind the way of the Father and the way of the Mother.

The incarnation of these Lightbearers was a cycling from the etheric plane to the mental plane to the emotional plane and finally to the physical density in which we now live. This incarnation occurred on Lemuria, and it came through the representative of the World Mother at that time, sponsored by the Manus, who were the sponsors of the root races.

The point of origin of the incarnation of the Lightbearers who came with Sanat Kumara is that half of them incarnate in the East and half in the West. Their incarnation is like the action of a caduceus, and the flame that they receive of the East or the West has to do with a specific endowment of an energy cycle for a certain period of their incarnations. It could be one; it could be seven; it could be a cycle of incarnations on an arc of that caduceus.

In the West, the Lightbearers who incarnate to serve the light are known as the twelve tribes of Israel. In the East, they form the mystery schools that are in the tradition of the Guru and the chela. In each instance, this body of souls is intended to pass on, generation to generation in an unbroken chain all the way from Lemuria, the true teachings of the religion of the Father and the religion of the Mother.

These Lightbearers have a more than ordinary initiation on the Path, hence they are called sons and daughters of God. The term "son of God" or "daughter of God" is a title, and it is an indication of a certain inner attainment, an initiation of the Christ that may have occurred even on other systems of worlds, long before the soul's descent to earth.

The term for other evolutions of God is "children of God." These have the same potential—they have the threefold flame, and they are begotten of the Father-Mother God. But they have not been in incarnation long enough to have attained a certain quotient of the light of Father, Son and Holy Spirit, a certain development of the threefold flame.

These sons and daughters of God have remained to this hour the ones who were ordained to represent the Ancient of Days as leaders in government, in religion, in science, in education—to set the example in all areas for the transfer of the culture that was once on Lemuria and now is held in trust on Venus.

Paths of East and West

The Lightbearers, then, are weaving a planetary caduceus: a certain series of embodiments in the East for the mastery of the five secret rays, a certain series of embodiments in the West for the mastery of the seven rays—back and forth, back and forth.

The center line of the caduceus is the yellow fire of the wisdom of the mind of God, the blue is the Father and the pink is the Mother. The religion of the Father and of the Mother are interpreted in East and West through the enlightened ones who are the Christ and the Buddha. The main streams of East and West are the Christ consciousness and the Buddhic consciousness. Thus, the initiation is to incarnate in both male and female bodies and to serve for the mastery of the masculine and feminine rays of the polarity of God in both of those bodies.

The characteristic of the path of the East has been the emphasis on the elimination of desire, inordinate desire. Gautama Buddha taught that desire creates entanglements and results in being tied to lower evolutions; it results in suffering, and the only way to be free from suffering is to be free from desire. Thus, in the East the way to end the cycles of incarnation is to achieve soul liberation, symbolized by the path of the Buddha.

In the West, the evolution of the twelve tribes under the Judeo-Christian tradition has been a history of disobedience and chastisement and then redemption. Recorded in the Old Testament, there is history of the judgment of the people of Israel delivered over and over again through laggard evolutions.

The quest in the West has centered around finding grace in the sight of God through the finding of the Christ, the Mediator, and through becoming the friend of God, as Abraham was a friend of God through that Christ.[2] This path is fulfilled in the person of Jesus Christ.

It is almost impossible to conceive that the people of great light of the East and the people of great light of the West could in any way be separated—and yet, this has occurred, and many people see a great gulf between the religions of East and West. Yet there is a certain group of people on earth who have an instantaneous awareness of the confluence of the River of Life in the Eastern and the Western tradition.

We may have grown up in a Western culture, and yet as soon as we have become aware of the teachings of Hinduism and Buddhism, we have immediately recognized ourselves to be inherently Buddhists or Hindus or Taoists. At the same time, we have the understanding of Judaism and Christianity, and this understanding is in our souls and is not necessarily that which is taught today. Thus, we see in our own lives the evidence of this caduceus action of the incarnation of the sons and daughters of God East and West.

The Twelve Tribes: Seed of Sanat Kumara and Abraham

The recorded history of these Lightbearers in the West, the twelve tribes of Israel, begins in the Bible, in Genesis, chapter 12, when God promises to bless Abraham: "I will make of thee a great nation, and I will bless thee, and make thy name great; and thou shalt be a blessing."[3]

In chapter 15 God says to Abraham (when he was still known as Abram): "Look now toward heaven, and tell the stars, if thou be able to number them: and he said unto him, So shall thy seed be."[4] God then told Abraham to make a sacrifice. He did so, and God told him of a karma that would come upon his seed:

"And when the sun was going down, a deep sleep fell upon Abram; and, lo, an horror of great darkness fell upon him. And [the LORD] said unto Abram, Know of a surety that thy seed shall be a stranger in a land that is not theirs, and shall serve them; and they shall afflict them four hundred years; and also that nation, whom they shall serve, will I judge: and afterward shall they come out with great substance. [This is a prophecy of the captivity of the twelve tribes in Egypt.]

"And thou shalt go to thy fathers in peace; thou shalt be buried in a good old age. But in the fourth generation they shall come hither again: for the iniquity of the Amorites is not yet full."5

Sanat Kumara chose Abraham to be the father of the Israelites, to be the one who would receive in his old age, through Sarah, the son Isaac. Isaac would then have the son Jacob; Jacob would give birth to twelve sons, who would become the progenitors of the twelve tribes.

Thus, Abraham is the great patriarch of the Lightbearers, chosen to bear the seed of Alpha. These souls came with a specific mission to be a witness unto the true God in the midst of idolatry, in the midst of the great darkness of the Middle East, such as that seen at Sodom and Gomorrah. They came to illustrate the blessedness of serving God, to receive and preserve the prophecy and the revelations, and above all, to be the channel through whom the Messiah would be born.

The Twelve Sons of Jacob

In approximately 1900 B.C. God conferred his blessing on Isaac, Abraham's son: "And the LORD appeared unto him the same night and said, I AM the God of Abraham thy father: fear not, for I am with thee, and will bless thee, and multiply thy seed for my servant Abraham's sake."6

It is very interesting that the LORD blesses each generation of Lightbearers, signifying that the blessing is not automatic by a transference of heredity, but comes by the reinstatement of the blessing for each generation.

Isaac's son Jacob received the LORD's blessing in his turn many years later: "And he dreamed, and behold a ladder set up on the earth, and the top of it reached to heaven: and behold the angels of God ascending and descending on it. And, behold, the LORD stood above it, and said, I AM the LORD God of Abraham thy father, and the God of Isaac: the land whereon thou liest, to thee will I give it, and to thy seed; and thy seed shall be as the dust of the earth . . . and in thy seed shall all the families of the earth be blessed."[7]

Jacob received another blessing when he wrestled with a "man" until the break of day and said, "I will not let thee go, except thou bless me." At the breaking of the day, he received the blessing: "Thy name shall be called no more Jacob, but Israel: for as a prince hast thou power with God and with men, and hast prevailed."[8] Jacob had wrestled with the angel, Archangel Michael, who purged him of his evil and thereby allowed him to receive the anointing of the name "Israel."

Jacob had twelve sons, born of his four wives. They were anointed by Sanat Kumara to carry the seed of light for the ultimate fulfillment of the destiny of the Lightbearers. His favorite son was the eleventh, Joseph. "Now Israel [Jacob] loved Joseph more than all his children, because he was the son of his old age: and he made him a coat of many colors."[9]

The coat of many colors is the symbol of the Causal Body of the children of Israel. He chose Joseph to wear this coat because he saw that Joseph had the greatest manifestation of the Christ consciousness and could carry the flame of the blending of all of the color rays of the Causal Body. So, Joseph received his birthright from his father, Israel.

But Joseph's brothers were jealous of him. They first plotted to kill him, but decided instead to sell him into slavery.

Joseph was taken to Egypt, where he gained the confidence of the Pharaoh and became second in command. When drought and famine besieged the land, Jacob and his eleven sons came to Egypt to find food. Joseph revealed himself to them, and the family was reunited. Once again the twelve brothers became united as one mandala.

As a token of his love for Joseph, Jacob took his two sons, Manasseh and Ephraim, for his own: "And now thy two sons, Ephraim and Manasseh, which were born unto thee in the land of Egypt before I came unto thee into Egypt, are mine; as Reuben and Simeon, they shall be mine."[10] Jacob prophesied to Joseph: "God shall be with you, and bring you again unto the land of your fathers."[11]

The names of the twelve sons of Jacob are Reuben, Simeon, Levi, Judah, Issachar, Zebulun, Joseph, Gad, Asher, Dan, Naphtali and Benjamin. The descendents of each son became the twelve tribes, and each tribe took the name of its patriarch. In earlier lists Joseph is named as one of the tribes. In later lists, Levi is omitted and Joseph is replaced by his sons, Ephraim and Manasseh. Levi thus became the thirteenth tribe, the one in the center of the circle holding the office of Christ and the flame of the priesthood.

Prior to his death, Jacob gave his final blessing to his twelve sons, and he gave his prophecy of the tribes and their destiny. It is recorded in Genesis, chapter 49.

Admonishment and Blessing of the Twelve Tribes

After many years, the descendants of Jacob's sons living in Egypt multiplied to such a degree that the Pharaoh felt threatened by their numbers and might. He enslaved them and ordered all newborn Hebrew males to be drowned at birth.

Moses was born during this perilous time, but his mother

saved his life by setting him afloat in a basket on the Nile. Pharaoh's daughter found him and raised him as her own son. In answer to a call from God, Moses led his people out of Egypt toward the Promised Land. After forty years of wandering in the wilderness, the Hebrews, under the leadership of Joshua, entered and conquered the Promised Land, the land of Canaan.

Joshua divided the conquered territory among the tribes according to God's direction. The only tribe that did not receive territory was the tribe of the Levites. The Levites led the people in worship, were responsible for teaching God's Law and performed other religious functions. The twelve tribes formed a loosely knit confederacy bonded together by their religious covenant with God. They were each in charge of their own territory, but in time of crisis they banded together to fight a common enemy.

Before his parting, Moses gives a blessing and an admonishment to these twelve tribes and the passing of the torch to his chela, Joshua. In these parting words, Moses rebukes them and prophesies that although he has admonished them to walk uprightly and to choose life and not death, they will backslide; they will become stiff-necked; they will forget his word as soon as he has departed. These words are recorded in the final chapters of Deuteronomy.

Moses commanded that the books of the Law, the first five books of the Bible, should be placed in the Ark of the Covenant along with this admonishment. And so he said, I will set this for a witness that I have delivered my message. I have put my message into a song, and when you read it, it will be for a judgment against you that you have gone against my laws and against my teachings.[12]

Moses warned them against mingling with the neighboring nations, taking up their gods, intermarrying with them. These neighboring nations were the nations of the Nephilim* and the fallen ones. And Moses predicted that they would enter into associations with them, walk in their ways and follow their idolatry. He predicted that if they did so, therefore choosing their cult of death, the curses of the Lord would be upon them—meaning that judgment, or karma, would come upon them for their actions.

At the conclusion of the reading is Moses' blessing of these twelve tribes before his transition. We see the great love of Sanat Kumara through Moses for each of those twelve tribes. Previously there had been the rebuke and the statement of karma and their faults. Yet in this blessing, each one is praised, and there is a prophecy given as to what they will accomplish. These prophecies are veiled and they are based on symbolism. The seal of that blessing gives us the divine plan and the opportunity for victory of each of these twelve tribes, as they each hold one line of the twelve points on our cosmic clock of initiation. (See pages 147–50.)

Moses was the Great Guru unto the twelve tribes of Israel. We are living in an hour when all of the promises of God through the prophets for the restoration of the memory of the tribes and the restoration of the Promised Land are about to be fulfilled—prophecies concerning the transmutation of karma couched in the words, "I will remember their sin no more."[13]

---

*Nephilim [Hebrew *Nephilim* 'those who fell' or 'those who were cast down,' from the Semitic root *naphal* 'to fall']: a biblical race of giants or demigods (Gen. 6:4). According to scholar Zecharia Sitchin, ancient Sumerian tablets depict the Nephilim as an extraterrestrial superrace who "fell" to earth in spacecraft 450,000 years ago. The ascended masters reveal that the Nephilim are the fallen angels cast out of heaven into the earth (Rev. 12:7–10, 12). See Zecharia Sitchin, *The Twelfth Planet* (New York: Avon Books, 1976).

The Dispersion

After Joshua passed on, the tribes were led by judges. The judges were primarily charismatic military leaders raised up by God to defend the people against the encroachments of neighboring nations.

During the period of the judges, from about 1200 to 1030 B.C., the Israelites began to worship pagan gods, the gods of materialism, the gods of the fallen angels. God punished them for their idolatry and apostasy by allowing other nations to harass and attack them. These invaders seized their land and crops and exacted tribute from them.

When the Israelites repented and obeyed God's laws, the LORD empowered the judges to champion their cause, and once again they enjoyed peace. The pattern of disobedience then punishment, repentance then deliverance was repeated over and over again. The leadership of the judges ended when the people demanded of Samuel, the last judge of Israel: "We will have a king over us that we also may be like all the nations."[14] They believed their tribal confederacy was not strong enough to ward off the growing threat of Philistine armies.

Samuel told the people that their desire for a king was a rejection of God. In fact, it showed a waning of their attunement with the living Presence of God with them and their forgetfulness of God's continual deliverance as he manifested himself to them through Archangel Michael, Archangel Gabriel and all of the heavenly hosts. And so, they looked for power in a human being, a leader and a king.

Samuel reluctantly consented to their demand by anointing Saul king but warned that a monarchy would bring them oppression. When Saul died, David became king of Israel after a short period during which Saul's son ruled over the northern tribes. Solomon succeeded his father, David, to the throne, and although he brought prosperity and peace to the land, he also placed a heavy burden on the people through taxation and slavery.

Shortly after Solomon's death in about 922 B.C., the ten tribes in the North rebelled against Solomon's son and successor to the throne, Rehoboam. These tribes formed their own kingdom, called Israel, ruled by their own king. The tribes of Judah and Benjamin made up the smaller and poorer Southern Kingdom, called Judah.

For about fifty years following the division of the kingdom, Israel and Judah fought a civil war over border territory. Partly as a result of their squabbles with each other, the two kingdoms lost territory to neighboring nations. In the coming centuries, Israel and Judah became more and more vulnerable because of their backsliding. The prophet Hosea, preaching in the Northern Kingdom, decried the growing social corruption, worship of pagan gods and moral decay. He warned the Israelites that they had broken their sacred covenant with God and would pay the price.

In 721 B.C. the Assyrians under Sargon II conquered the Northern Kingdom of Israel and forcibly deported most of the people to Assyria. This was the end of the Northern Kingdom. Because the fate of the ten northern tribes after they were deported is unknown, they are referred to as the ten lost tribes. It is widely believed that they never again returned to their homeland.

With the demise of the Northern Kingdom, Judah became a vassal of Assyria, and then, in the seventh century B.C., it became a vassal of the Babylonian Empire. During this turbulent time, the prophet Jeremiah preached God's imminent judgment upon Judah for her sinfulness. He warned that if the people did not turn wholeheartedly to their God, they would meet the same fate as Israel at the hands of an "evil from the north."[15]

Judah, like Israel, was guilty of idolatry, apostasy, corruption and moral degeneracy. They had erected altars to a host of foreign gods whom they worshiped alongside the LORD. The fertility cult's sacred prostitution was practiced in the Temple at Jerusalem. Some of the people even took part in the pagan practice of human sacrifice, making "their sons and their daughters to pass through the fire unto Molech."[16]

The LORD's prophecy through Jeremiah was fulfilled. The king of Judah rebelled against the Babylonians, and in 597 B.C. the Babylonian king Nebuchadnezzar besieged Jerusalem and deported the king and leading men of Judah.

In 587 B.C., the Babylonians totally destroyed Jerusalem—looting, burning every building including the Temple, and deporting all but a few inhabitants. A third deportation took place in 582 B.C. Although they had been taken from their homeland, the conditions for the exiles were not unfavorable. The Jews became farmers, merchants, traders, soldiers, even government officials, some rising to positions of wealth.

The Coming of the Messiah

In 538 B.C. the Persian king Cyrus, conqueror of Babylonia, issued a decree permitting the Jews to return to Jerusalem and rebuild the Temple. Most of them had forgotten and were not concerned with their inheritance; only a small remnant of the tribes returned, most of them from the tribes of Judah and Benjamin. They brought the Temple vessels that had been stripped from them in 587 B.C., and the Temple in Jerusalem was rebuilt.

This was the time of preparation for the coming of the Messiah. As we now understand, the preparation for Jesus' coming had begun with Sanat Kumara, Abraham, Isaac, Jacob, the twelve sons. But what happened to them?

Living at this particular period in Egypt and in the Fertile Crescent were a conglomeration of peoples. Some of them were Baal worshipers, worshipers of Ashtaroth. They were a laggard generation, descendants of Atlantis. They were the ones who condemned the prophets, who rejected Noah, who mocked him.

And amidst these laggards who had come from other spheres, who had lagged behind their planetary evolutions, there was born a people of great light, people who had come with Sanat Kumara, people who were of the angelic hosts. They were mingled all together in the Fertile Crescent, and the great patriarchs and the prophets were constantly trying to draw the people of light out from among the people of darkness. They were even given the decree that they should not intermarry with those who worshiped idols and other gods. And they were constantly reminded of who their God was.

But they did not heed their teachers and prophets. There was the mingling of the seed of light and darkness—the very same thing we see today in every nation on earth. They were overcome by the Serpent. They sinned. They rebelled against God. Therefore, they lacked the community and the physical focus of the Great White Brotherhood.

What was left was a tiny remnant of Lightbearers, and so, instead of coming into the kingdom of Israel, Jesus was born under the Roman Empire. Immediately facing the persecution of Herod, he and his family had to flee to Egypt.

Jesus came as a lone avatar, and he had to stand against the entire Babylon of Church and the Babylon of State. He stood against the priesthood that had invaded the people of Israel, that had destroyed the real essence of the teaching of Moses and Sanat Kumara.

Because they had already lost their true race and had

mingled with the peoples of Canaan and of the Fertile Crescent, most of the twelve tribes had compromised their own Christ consciousness given to them by their prophets. Therefore, they could not recognize the Christ in Jesus.

Nevertheless, he came, and when he raised up his apostles and gave them his mantle to go after the lost sheep of the house of Israel,[17] he was sending them to find the Lightbearers of the lost tribes, those who had lost their identity, forgotten who they were and were now scattered abroad. He sent them throughout Asia Minor. They went as far as India and Italy. They went throughout the entire known world, searching for the Lightbearers.

The Twelve Tribes Today

In his book *The Human Aura,* the Ascended Master Djwal Kul takes up the story of the twelve tribes and traces their destiny to the present day.

"My beloved, hear now the story of the bondage of the souls of the Israelites, how they were freed by God from the Egyptian bondage and how they entered again into the bondage of the fleshpots of Egypt.

"So great was the abomination of those who had been chosen to bear the Word of the Law that the LORD God allowed them to be taken into Assyrian and Babylonian captivity and ultimately to be scattered over the face of the earth. Those among the descendants of the twelve tribes of Israel who remembered their calling to free a planet and her people from idolatry and who had never compromised the law of the prophets and the patriarchs were allowed to embody upon a new continent. They were given another land that was the fulfillment of the promise of God unto Abraham, the land of the I AM race.

"That race is composed of all peoples and kindreds and tongues who have the worship of the individual Christ and the one God, the God of Abraham, of Isaac and of Jacob, who declared himself unto Moses as the principle of the I AM THAT I AM, and who affirmed, 'This is my name for ever, and this is my memorial unto all generations.'[18]

"Because the original race that was chosen to bear that name compromised the light, the very Christos of the seed of the patriarchs, the opportunity to bear the flame of freedom was widened to include all who would choose to come apart from the idolatrous generation, to be a separate people, who would raise up in the wilderness of the human consciousness the brazen serpent,[19] which symbolized the raising up of the energies of the Divine Mother, the serpentine fires of the Goddess Kundalini. This is indeed the caduceus action rising as the life force, the energy that blossomed as Aaron's rod through the union of the spirals of Alpha and Omega."[20]

What happened to the twelve tribes? They were scattered across the face of the earth following the ministry of Jeremiah.

The ten northern tribes have reincarnated among those who have been called the Gentiles. Some have sought to trace physically the migration of these tribes to Europe, Russia and the British Isles. They trace the origins of the shields and crests of the different cities and states to those of the twelve tribes, whose emblems are derived from the final blessing Jacob gave his sons. They also see the prophecies of Jacob and Moses about the different tribes fulfilled in the history of different European nations.[21] Whether the tracing is proven through a physical lineage or not, we do know that they remained intact as a soul mandala. They have descended, many of them walking according to the Christian faith, accepting the Messiah and yet forgetting their origin as members of those ten tribes.

The tribes of Judah and Benjamin in the south and some of

the Levites who were with them remembered they were Jews but did not perceive the fulfillment of the prophecy of the coming of Messiah.

The members of the twelve tribes are Sanat Kumara's legions. They have been carrying this flame of the true Israel through all the mystery schools, through Camelot, through the school at Crotona, through the ashrams of India and Asia. Everywhere there has been a nucleus of Lightbearers and the acknowledgment of the Source and the Mediator (The I AM THAT I AM and the Christ), there has been the gathering, once again, of the Israelites scattered over the face of the earth as the seed of Abraham, which became the seed of Christ through David.

The Bible is a record of how these souls who came through Abraham succeeded and how they failed. The twelve tribes have an assignment, and they are born to deal with a certain energy. We see that their failure throughout the Old Testament until their final dispersion is based on the fact that they have not seized this assignment and fulfilled it.

This is the karma that we have today, as we have inherited the karma of those twelve tribes. As the Lightbearers, the ones who bear the seed of light, we have the responsibility for the transmutation of everything we read in the Old and the New Testaments.

Our mission today is to realize who we are, where we fit into the mandala of these twelve tribes and then to balance the karma that the twelve tribes have made. In balancing that karma through the violet flame, through our invocations, we eliminate the forcefields, the islands of darkness that keep the tribes separated and also keep the members of each tribe separated from one another. The burden of this karma is why the tribes have no sense of identity today, and the real members of the tribes have no idea who they are.

Jesus Christ took embodiment to go after the lost sheep of the house of Israel, those who had lost their memory of having ever been part of the light of Sanat Kumara. And we, today, are a remnant of those tribes. The Lightbearers incarnating in every age in East and West are the very same members of the twelve tribes of Israel.

Old Testament prophecy, then, is our heritage. Coming out of Egypt, crossing over the Red Sea, going into the Promised Land and then being disobedient and being chastised—all of this is what we have gone through collectively in our incarnations of the West.

The New World, Promised Land for the Gathering of the Twelve Tribes

As we trace the history of the reincarnated tribes, we find a very special destiny for the sons of Joseph and the two tribes of Ephraim and Manasseh. These two sons of Joseph, having the highest blessing, the very personal blessing of Jesus Christ in the person of Joseph,* having his seed, are the ones called to reverse the sin of the other brothers of the house of Jacob. The other brothers had great sins in their day and unto the present hour.

We also see in Joseph that he married the daughter of an Egyptian priest, and therefore the seed of Egypt and of the ancient Pharaohs, even coming down from Ikhnaton and Nefertiti and the religion of monotheism, is among these particular tribes. They went to the British Isles and became the nucleus of the English-speaking people in Britain, America and the world.

It was given to them to carry the cup of the Christ consciousness and to bring the English language all over the world through colonization and through discovery, so that when the

---

*Jesus was embodied as Joseph, the son of Jacob.

teachings of the I AM THAT I AM would be given again to the children of Israel, they would come through the English language, the language chosen because it most nearly reflected the angelic tongue that is the source of the original teaching to the original people of Israel. So it was the destiny, then, of the English-speaking peoples to carry that Christ consciousness to the new world.

The new world, America, is the land that was promised by the LORD God to the children of Israel. They were told that they would be brought into a new land and would be given a new dispensation. Early records in the history of the nation show that the founding fathers of America knew that they were the people of Israel, that they were the inheritors of this promise and that they had come to a new world to found the New Israel, the New Jerusalem, the new mystery school, the new place of dispensation. We see this symbolized in the Great Seal of the United States, with the All-Seeing Eye of God in the capstone of the pyramid, focalizing the mission of the twelve tribes.

Even in the name, America, there is revealed the origin and destiny of the nation. The letters of the name, when rearranged, spell I AM Race. This is the race of the children of Israel who have accepted their God-reality, who know God as the I AM that was revealed to Moses.[22] They have been called to America as the gathering together of the elect from the four winds,[23] from the four corners of the earth, to bring forth the Christ consciousness and then to take that Christ consciousness to every nation. This is the mission of the Israelites in the United States, founded upon the mystery school of the thirteen—thirteen founding states, Christ and his apostles.

So we see the emigration, vast lines of pilgrims, first from the British Isles, the brothers Manasseh and Ephraim, and then from the tribes of all the different European nations becoming the foundation of the United States.

Tracing the Seed of Light

We go back, then, to the very history of Jacob and the coming of the twelve tribes to discover our own history. As we understand our history, we understand our blessing. When we study the promises of the prophets and the patriarchs to us, then, when we give our invocations, we are standing upon the rock of Christ, and we have the confirmation of the Word through the flame of the Ark of the Covenant.

These tribes have a destiny to fulfill. That destiny is to unite under the banner of the I AM THAT I AM—the Presence of God individualized in each one of us in whom there burns the flame of God. Through the Spirit of the living Christ, we are destined to become a major world power.

The twelve tribes of Israel today are not a lineage of twelve tribes by blood, but their descent can best be explained by reincarnation. The seed of Abraham was scattered. They continued to reembody, always carrying that seed, and therefore, they may not be in bodies that resemble the Semite people. They may very well be Chinese or African or Indian or any race. But they have come again.

The seed that they carry is the nucleus of the Christ consciousness. All who have the Christ consciousness are of this seed. And you find that there is a dividing line. You find people of every religion who deny that Flame, that essence, that Spirit, and deny the opportunity for the individual to become that Christ. Others have known from the beginning that they were Christ, they were that Flame, they were that Reality. Others have known it by another name and have intensely resisted the name Christ, but when they understand the true meaning, then they realize that that is the indwelling Presence with whom they, also, have communed.

In the seventh chapter of the Book of Revelation, we read

the prophecy of the sealing of the servants of God in their foreheads, twelve thousand from each of the twelve tribes, a total of 144,000. They also appear in chapter 14 as those gathered around the throne of the Lamb, who is Sanat Kumara. And so, in Revelation there is a continuing chronicle of the twelve tribes and of their overcoming of all that is revealed.

Our Destiny as the Twelve Tribes

The twelve tribes of Israel have not maintained a continuous identity over these thousands of years. But our great victory lies in the fact that the identity is in the Inner Flame; no one can take from us the flame of light, the Flame of God, the original Word, the memory of the teachings of East and West, the instantaneous rapport with the I AM THAT I AM and the recognition that Christ was not alone in Jesus but that he is in us. When you find people that have that awareness, you are finding the members of the house of Israel and Judah.

The genius of the twelve tribes is in every nation. All of the nations are forcefields for the development of the Christ consciousness through the twelve tribes, and each of the nations of the earth is an opportunity for the Lightbearers to master a certain initiation of a certain chakra.

We find today that the twelve tribes have been caught up and lost their identity as the tribes of Israel and have identified themselves now within their many nations. They have not realized that they have put on their nationhood to identify in that nation, to set the example of the lightbearer to the people.

The Ascended Master Saint Patrick has come to help us make contact with the Lightbearers of all nations, to alert them to the message, to alert them to the teachings of the Ascended Masters, to bring them together so that they can form the nucleus for the victory and the salvation of earth. Until we make this contact, identify our brotherhood, identify our community, we do not sense our strength.

He has said: "I AM the defender of the Woman in this age. I come, then, to secure a place for her children—children of the Mother who have come out of the land of Israel so long ago that they have forgotten their source and their common origin as the seed of Abraham, of David and of Christ, the Messiah of all.

"I come, then, to deliver the mandate of truth, and it is this, that the children of the light must be one, that all who have gone forth out of the nucleus of the sacred fire of Jerusalem to the four corners of the earth now are called to be sons and daughters of God. And yet they remain as prisoners of their respective nations—prisoners in the sense that they are bound by certain customs and laws and political and religious ideologies, whereby they have forgotten the one true law of the I AM THAT I AM.

"I center, then, the energies of the fiery core of my being here in the heart of the city, the New Jerusalem, and I place the magnet of my devotion to the Mother for the calling in of the rays of the house of the Lord, the rays of Ikhnaton, who saw the one God and the people of God as one, the rays that will call back the one hundred and forty-four thousand flames of the twelve tribes of Israel. . . . [24]

"All of this warfare and this division that has been created as the divide-and-conquer tactic of the fallen ones, even midst the brethren of Ireland and of the British Commonwealth of Nations and throughout Europe and the Eastern countries, all of this is to this one purpose, children of the Light—now understand it is to keep the children of Israel separate and apart in the last days.

"For in every nation there are Lightbearers. But the fallen ones and those who have never elected to be one with the light of God, these live also among these nations. And the children of God, instead of identifying with the life and the Body and the Blood of Christ, have begun to identify themselves as members of these nations. And therefore, they see their national loyalties as greater than their loyalty to the one purpose of the Ancient of Days, Sanat Kumara, which was to keep the flame of life for the evolutions of this earth.

"See, then, that you understand that for the defense of the karma and the dharma of the people among whom you have embodied, you must call yourself an American, an Italian, a Chinese or a Russian, but for the purposes of the salvation of earth, you must understand yourselves as the deliverers of the nations.

"The cutting free of the nations by the action of your sword of life is your mission and your goal. It is to free the nations to behold within themselves, and not to come under, then, the boot and the darkness of those who proclaim a one-world government and yet do it not in the name of Christ, but in the name of a scientific humanism.

"They do err, and their divide-and-conquer tactics have taken a new course in this age. It is to play upon the reality of the inner understanding of the people of God that indeed the earth is one, and to carry that understanding into a perversion whereby the karma and the dharma of the people of the nations is destroyed as they are forced to come into a totalitarian system whereby they are divested of their natural genius and their calling from the mansions of the Father's house....

"I am of the house of Israel! I am of one of the twelve tribes! I come to return the tribes to the one God! I come to rescue all who have gone out of the way! I come as the instrument of the Cosmic Virgin to support the work of the World Mother and her emissaries in this age."[25]

FIGURE 3: THE MISSION OF THE TWELVE TRIBES

FIGURE 3A: The Twelve Solar Hierarchies

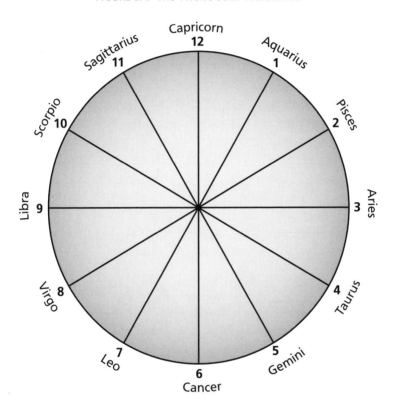

The twelve tribes came to planet Earth with the mission to bear the light of the Twelve Hierarchies of the Sun, twelve mandalas of cosmic beings ensouling twelve facets of God's consciousness, who hold the pattern of that frequency for the entire cosmos. They are identified by the names of the signs of the zodiac, as they focus their energies through these constellations. They are diagrammed as lines of a clock, with Capricorn on the twelve o'clock line, Aquarius on the one, and so on.

[For more information on the Twelve Solar Hierarchies, see book 3 in the *Climb the Highest Mountain* series, *The Masters and the Spiritual Path*.]

FIGURE 3B:
The Twelve Tribes on the Twelve Lines of the Clock

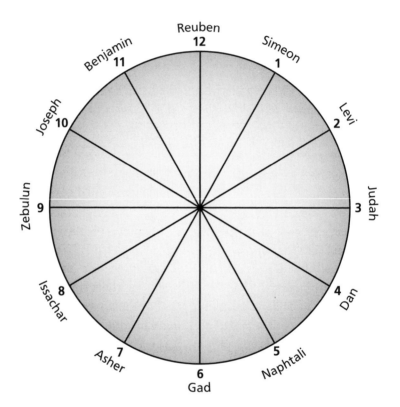

The tribes are placed on the clock according to the birth order of the twelve sons of Jacob.

FIGURE 3C:
The God Consciousness, or God-Qualities of the Solar Hierarchies

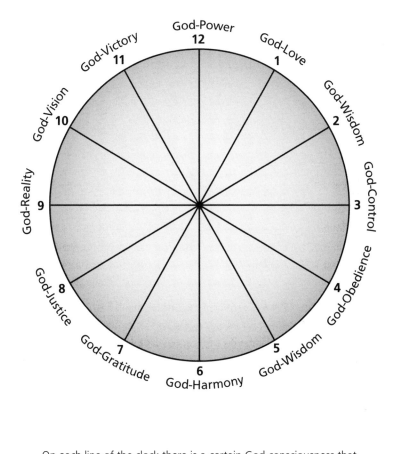

On each line of the clock there is a certain God consciousness that is ensouled by that Hierarchy and is intended to be held in the earth by that tribe. There is also a negative quality of each line, representing the misuse of the energy of that Hierarchy and the specific karma that needs to be transmuted on that line.

According to our own birth sign, we can pursue the manifestation within our own lives of the God consciousness of that Hierarchy; we can also call for the transmutation of the karma of that line. By doing this, we can identify with the mission of one of the tribes and assist in its fulfillment.

FIGURE 3D:

Negative Karma to Be Transmuted on Each Line of the Clock

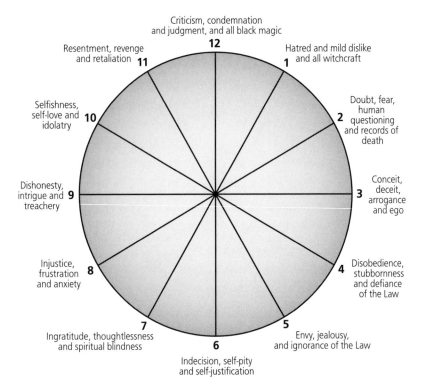

The Twelve Apostles

*Follow me, and I will make you
fishers of men.*

The Twelve Apostles

S AINT GERMAIN HAS EXPLAINED THAT the Matter universe and the Spirit universe are not separate, but one. Matter is not truly dense, but in fact, at the white-fire core of every atom there is a pulsation of energy from Spirit to Matter in such rapid motion that we no longer see it, and we think it is simply concrete matter. There is a flow of energy and a movement of energy; and that energy becomes the structure and the foundation of all true building in these planes.

In the Causal Body we see the pattern of the seven bands of the color rays: the inner rings that are at a different dimension, the five secret rays and the white-fire core. The five and the seven make twelve, the center thirteen. We see the basic outline of this atom of being in the Great Central Sun, which is the center of our cosmos, with all the galaxies revolving about it. And we find that the individualization of that same atom over and over again becomes a replica of the one light, the one God, the one Truth. Hence, in time and space we see repeated, from the tiniest particle of energy to our solar system, this basic principle of life.

FIGURE 4: The Twelve Spheres of the Causal Body

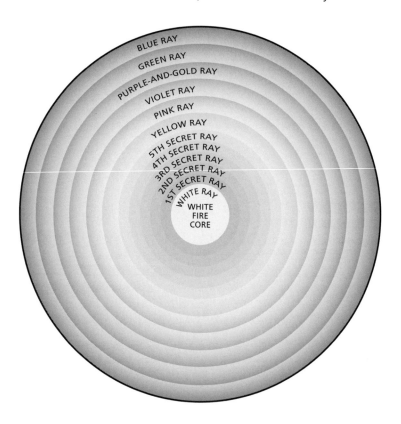

We see the same principle in Jesus' twelve apostles with Jesus holding the focus of the Christ consciousness in the center. This mandala is the archetypal pattern of Christ-mastery. The story of the apostles is interesting, and their service with Jesus is clear, even though we know little about them.

Our Calling to Be Apostles

It was on the foundation of the apostles and the prophets that the Christian Church was built, with Jesus Christ himself as the chief cornerstone. The distinction between the two is that, while the prophet was God's spokesman to the believing Church, the apostle was his envoy to the unbelieving world. Prophets are the lawgivers; they are God's spokesmen. It is to unbelievers, to those who know not the Christ within, that the apostle must have the courage to preach. There are many more apostles than prophets in the true Church, and we are all called to be apostles.

There is a pattern and a blueprint for the twelve apostles. They occupy positions in the cosmic hierarchy that we need to understand. Just as we are all born under one hierarchy of the sun, one of the signs of astrology, so we are born to fulfill the mission of one of the original twelve apostles.

The apostles gathered around Jesus to support the mission of the Christ consciousness. They had elected to do so at inner levels; they had been appointed and anointed by God. This is why, when Jesus called them, they immediately left their nets and followed him. When they heard the call, they knew his voice from the training they had in etheric temples. The entire life of Jesus had been rehearsed in the temples of light; he and his apostles came into embodiment to set forth the patterns in the physical plane.

The twelve apostles came forth to represent twelve cosmic hierarchies* around the central sun who was Christ Jesus, the one who showed forth all twelve aspects of the Christ consciousness and therefore had passed the initiations to stand in the center of the circle. The Christ standing in the center as the thirteenth holds the balance for all of the twelve. The Christ

---

*See diagrams, pp. 147–50.

must have the mastery of all twelve lines.

You, individually, may attain the Christ consciousness without having full and total mastery of every facet of every line. However, in order to have the attainment of the Buddha, you must have the full attainment of all lines. Jesus, for his mission for setting the pattern for the two-thousand-year cycle of Pisces, had that attainment. He was almost karma-free, as he had balanced most of his karma in previous lives. And yet he said, "Touch me not; for I am not yet ascended to my Father,"[1] meaning that his atoms, his electrons, his molecules were not yet perfected in the Flame, were not yet sealed in the permanent consciousness of the ascension spiral.

The twelve and the thirteenth is the basic pattern, or mandala, for every spiritual group. Although the group may be larger, there is always the one teacher who holds the focus in the center, and all the disciples become facets of the consciousness of God on the twelve lines of the clock.

Those who are passing initiations on the circle may pass the test of only one of the hierarchies at a time. We are each born under the sign of the hierarchy that gives us that initiation in the Christ consciousness, and so, we each are intended to bear the mantle of one of the apostles according to the astrological sign under which we are born.

The Mission of the Twelve Apostles

The Masters El Morya, Hilarion and Jesus have given us the key to where the apostles fall on the twelve lines of the clock. Whether or not they are embodied or ascended at this time, whether they passed or failed their tests at the time of Jesus, the Causal Body of each of these apostles contains the grid that is the pattern of the twelve for the Piscean age.

Only one of Jesus' apostles ascended at the conclusion of

that lifetime. John was the disciple who had the greatest love, and by love he conquered all with Christ. The other apostles reembodied, and some have continued to reincarnate until this century. Therefore, we see a new meaning of Jesus' command, "Tarry ye in the city of Jerusalem until ye be endued with power from on high."[2] They have tarried two thousand years in Matter, waiting for the coming of the Holy Ghost.

Some were required to reembody to carry the pattern of Jesus' mission in succeeding centuries and ages. Some of them had a mission to fulfill in the twentieth century; and they could not ascend because their blueprint, their divine plan had not been fulfilled. Others continued to reincarnate through willfulness, stubbornness, resistance of the Christ, and they continue to make karma and to have karma to balance.

If we desire to be a disciple of Jesus Christ, to follow him all the way, we will have a position on the clock around Jesus. As we determine our astrological sign, we will see the mission of the apostle who stood on that line and how he passed his tests or failed his tests. We can call for the Causal Body of that apostle to be superimposed over our own consciousness so that we can receive the gift of his mission.

Concern yourself with apostleship. Concern yourself with being worthy to be apostles for Christ. Accelerate your path of initiation. Go in to the fiery core of your own Christ consciousness. Put your house in order. Bring yourself into alignment with the sacred Word. Be God where you are. Speak with authority as Jesus did, and not as the scribes.[3] We do not want to be scribes and Pharisees. We want to be apostles for Christ.

It does not matter whether or not the apostle on your line of the clock has ascended, because it is an office in hierarchy, and it is the momentum of the Causal Body and the mantle of the God Flame of that apostle that comes upon you. The calling is to fulfill the office of that apostle where that apostle has failed and to fulfill the office where the apostle has succeeded.

We will outline here the lives of the apostles, what they did before and after Jesus' mission and their positions under the hierarchies so you can study these apostles, their lives, their weaknesses and their strengths.

FIGURE 5:
The Four Quadrants of the Cosmic Clock

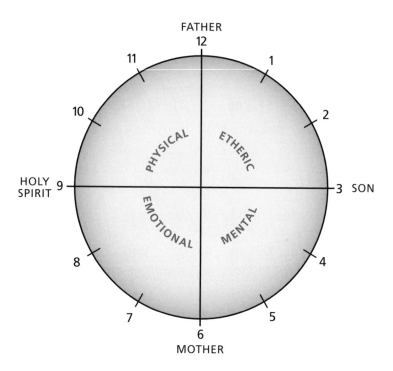

Each quadrant of the Cosmic Clock of the Twelve Solar Hierarchies corresponds to one of the four planes of Matter.

Andrew

The first disciple of Jesus was Andrew.[4] He was a fisherman, born in Bethsaida on the north shore of the Sea of Galilee. He and John the Evangelist were disciples of John the Baptist. John pointed out Jesus to them with the words "Behold the Lamb of God!"[5] Andrew followed Jesus, recognized him as the Messiah and returned home to tell his brother, Simon Peter. Later, Jesus approached Andrew and Peter, John and his brother James, on the shore and said, "Follow me, and I will make you fishers of men." They all immediately left their nets and followed him.[6] These four, who were the first to follow Jesus, formed a cube, holding the four cardinal points.

When, at his baptism, Jesus received the benediction "Thou art my beloved Son, in whom I am well pleased,"[7] this was the lowering of the etheric design of his mission. Andrew, as a disciple of John the Baptist, was present and received the etheric pattern. He is on the twelve o'clock line under the hierarchy of Capricorn, the beginning of the etheric quadrant.

Peter is on the three o'clock line, the sign of Aries. James is on the six o'clock line, the sign of Cancer and the line of the Mother. John the Beloved, the one of all the twelve who ascended, is the one who holds the focus of the Holy Spirit on the nine o'clock line. Because John was the victor on that line, Christianity has survived. He made Christianity tangible and set the perfect pattern in the physical plane. The City Foursquare is built on the Christ consciousness of these four.

Peter, James, and John are often thought of as the main disciples. They are on the lines of the mental, emotional and physical quadrants of the clock, which are the planes of outer awareness. People don't see God until God enters the mental plane. (In the same way, they don't see God as an etheric pattern. People think that the zodiac starts with Aries because

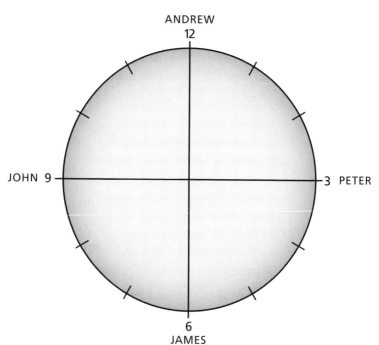

FIGURE 6:
The Apostles on the Cardinal Points of the Clock

that is the first place where they have an awareness.) And so that trinity of the threefold flame is made known to us in Peter, James and John. They are often known as the inner circle, but we should not exclude Andrew from that circle, because he is the fourth point that makes the cube that is necessary for the precipitation from Spirit to Matter.

The one who carries the etheric pattern for a mission and an organization and for a two-thousand-year period is not necessarily the key figure, although sometimes he may be. But this person has to be there because he carries in his Causal Body the etheric design. If you were born under the sign of Capricorn, you are intended to carry an etheric pattern for some facet of bringing the kingdom of God upon earth.

According to tradition, Andrew preached the gospel in Asia Minor, Macedonia, Greece and Southern Russia. The non-canonical Acts of Andrew describes his martyrdom at Patras in Greece by order of the Roman governor; the traditional date is November 30, A.D. 60. He was bound to a cross shaped like an X, and this is the origin of the Saint Andrew's cross in the British flag today. He is the patron saint of Russia and Scotland.

Philip

Philip was also born in Bethsaida, the city of Andrew and Peter. He is the apostle on the one o'clock line of Aquarius. John's gospel records that after calling Peter and Andrew, Jesus met Philip, and said to him, "Follow me." Philip, recognizing the Messiah, forsook all to follow Jesus and soon brought his friend Nathanael to see the Master.[8]

Eusebius, the early Church historian, relates that Philip preached the gospel in Phrygia in Asia Minor and was martyred at Hieropolis.

Thomas

On the two o'clock line, it was the office of Thomas to overcome the records of doubt, fear, human questioning and records of death. He had a great desire to lay down the human consciousness, to die and to let the Christ appear. When Jesus announced his intention to return to Judea to visit Lazarus, it was Thomas who said to his fellow disciples: "Let us also go, that we may die with him."[9] He is said to have been a carpenter, and his name in Syriac means "twin"; Didymus, as he was also known, is the Greek equivalent.

Thomas is most well-known for his expression of doubt in Jesus' resurrection. Thomas wanted to believe, but he stood in the place where the entire world momentum of fear, doubt, human questioning and records of death were being projected at Jesus. Jesus had the full mastery over those forces, but the apostles around him did not. As the intense waves of planetary opposition came in, those who were standing on the circle, if they could not raise their consciousness high enough, would begin to identify with that human consciousness instead of with the God consciousness of God-mastery on their line of the clock. And so, there are recorded the famous words of Thomas: "Except I shall see in his hands the print of the nails, and put my finger into the print of the nail, and thrust my hand into his side, I will not believe."

Eight days later Jesus appeared in their midst, and he said to Thomas: "Reach hither thy finger, and behold my hands; and reach hither thy hand, and thrust it into my side: and be not faithless, but believing." Whereupon Thomas prostrated himself and uttered the expression: "My Lord and my God." Jesus reproved him for his previous unbelief. "Because thou hast seen me, thou hast believed: blessed are they that have not seen, and yet have believed."[10]

It was necessary for Jesus to have the world momentum of doubt personified, so that the great drama of this conversation could be recorded and so that forevermore those who would doubt and fall into the trap of the two o'clock line would have the record that someone *had* doubted, someone had put his hands on Jesus, and really seen that there were holes and nail prints and a wound in the side. By that act, the record is set for all time, and that doubt is forevermore challenged. Jesus challenges that doubt in all of us and in all of the planet.

According to early traditions Thomas went forth after Jesus' ascension to teach the gospel of Christ in Babylon, India,

Parthia, Media and Persia. In India he instructed the people in the Christian religion and converted many kings and emperors. He performed numerous miracles, which won the hearts of the people but caused violent anger among the priests of the idols. In consequence, he was condemned to death and pierced with arrows.

Jesus has said of Thomas, "I invite each and every one of you . . . to become my twin, as my beloved apostle Thomas was my twin in that he did embody that Christ."[11]

Peter

Peter is on the three o'clock line, the line of the Son, the second person of the Trinity. This is the hierarchy of Aries and the hierarchy of the mind. It is always the key position in the building of the Church. Peter had to be the rock, he had to be the one upon whose shoulders Jesus placed the responsibilities of the early Church. No matter what his human consciousness or frailties, he was the one standing on the three o'clock line. He would rise or fall, but he would have to be there for that particular dispensation.

On the very first meeting Jesus had with Peter, he addressed him thus: "Thou art Simon the son of Jona: thou shall be called Cephas," the Aramaic word for "a stone."[12] Peter left his wife and mother-in-law to follow Jesus.

Later in the gospel account we read the account of Simon receiving the name Peter.

> [Who] do men say that I the Son of man am?
>
> And they said, Some say that thou art John the Baptist: some, Elias; and others, Jeremias, or one of the prophets.
>
> He saith unto them, But whom say ye that I am?
>
> And Simon Peter answered and said, Thou art the

Christ, the Son of the living God.

And Jesus answered and said unto him, Blessed art thou, Simon Barjona: for flesh and blood hath not revealed it unto thee, but my Father which is in heaven.

And I say also unto thee, That thou art Peter, and upon this rock I will build my church; and the gates of hell shall not prevail against it.[13]

Jesus is saying that the foundation of the Church is in the individual recognition of Jesus as the Son of God and of the Christ—the Anointed One, the one anointed by the sacred fire, by the Almighty One.* Jesus tells us that this recognition will not come by flesh and blood. Although Peter had been with him from the beginning, it was not the flesh and blood of the Master that revealed it, but the oneness of the Flame and of the consciousness.

If we, individually, would be the true Church, we must know that the very first white cube, the first stone, must be the recognition, by the power of the Holy Spirit, that Jesus is Christ the Lord; that Jesus, the Son of God who is and was and forever shall be Christ the Lord, is also alive within us. And because he is alive within us, that Christ within us is the same Christ, the same yesterday and today and forever.[14]

Mother Mary has explained the significance of these words of Jesus. "It is upon the rock of the individual Christ Self of every member of the Mystical Body of God and not upon the flesh-and-blood consciousness of Peter or of his successor that the rising or the falling of the Church must rest. Would we, then, place something so divine as the institution in heaven and on earth of the Mystical Body of God in the fragile chalice of the human will or human frailty? I tell you nay!

---

*The origin of the word "Christ" is the Greek *Christos*, "the Anointed."

"The Rock of the Church lives today in the hearts of those who are its true saints both within and without its ranks East and West and even those who may be devotees of Zarathustra or of the Lord Confucius. For that Body, which consists of the true and the faithful ones of God, is truly that Universal Church that maintains oneness in the Spirit with the Lord Jesus Christ and the saints in heaven. And that name, the name of the living Saviour, as the rose by any other name that smells as sweet, must be perceived as something vastly more cosmic and universal than the mere manifestation of the Christ by a single individual, even though that individual be the World Saviour and his name be Jesus.... Let the individual recognize himself as the living Church. For not a cathedral nor an institution but a heart that beats one with the heart of God—this is my definition of Church."[15]

Jesus was very concerned about Peter because he knew the pitfalls of the three o'clock line, which is the line of the ego. If people do not overcome the human aspect, or the human consciousness of Aries, they go the way of Lucifer, who fell on the three o'clock line through his intellectual pride. Jesus knew that the Church depended upon Peter passing this test.

In the Biblical account, Jesus spoke more often to Peter than to any other of his disciples, both in blaming and in praise. Jesus said to Peter: "Satan hath desired to have you, that he may sift you as wheat."[16] He also told Peter that he would betray him ere the cock crew three times, and Peter did deny him three times when asked if he was one of Jesus' followers. Peter had great remorse for this.[17]

There was one redeeming factor about Peter's character, and that was his exquisite sense of sin. He was extremely sensitive and tender in his spirit in this respect. It was Peter who said: "Depart from me; for I am a sinful man, O Lord."[18]

At the end of his life Peter was leaving Rome, fleeing

persecution and his own martyrdom. However, it was not God's will that he should leave the flock in Rome. As he was walking along the Appian Way, Jesus appeared in the road before him, and Peter's eyes were bedazzled when he saw the figure of his Lord. He looked up and said the famous words: "Quo Vadis, Domine?" "Where are you going, Lord?" Jesus answered, "I am going to Rome to be crucified again."

By this Peter knew that he must return to Rome to be crucified for Jesus. He went back, and in his humility and love for Jesus, he requested that he not be crucified as Jesus was but that he be crucified upside down. He was martyred in the circus of Gaius and Nero, and St. Peter's Basilica was built on the site of his tomb.

We can say as the summation of Peter's life that he did fall short of the mark in many respects in mastering the three o'clock line of God-control. It is a certain aspect of those who come under the sign of Aries to be impetuous and impatient—and this Peter was. As we read his story in the Bible, we also see his great devotion to Jesus and the mission. His preaching and his miracles feature prominently in the Book of Acts and are a testimony to the power of the Spirit working through him.

Bartholomew

Bartholomew (known as Nathanael in the fourth gospel) is on the four o'clock line of Taurus. After Philip had been called by Jesus, he immediately told his friend Nathanael: "We have found him, of whom Moses in the law, and the prophets, did write, Jesus of Nazareth, the son of Joseph." Bartholomew at first was skeptical about the Saviour: "Can there any good thing come out of Nazareth?" Philip answered: "Come and see." And he went and saw, and Nathanael also became a disciple. As soon as Jesus saw Nathanael, he said: "Behold, an

Israelite indeed, in whom is no guile!"[19]

According to early traditions, Bartholomew took the teachings of Christ to Egypt, Phrygia, Persia, India and Armenia. He preached with such success that the heathen gods were rendered powerless. He met his death as a martyr in Armenia.

Matthew

On the five o'clock line is Matthew, also called Levi. He was a tax collector for the Romans, and as such he would have been educated and acquainted with the Aramaic, the Greek and Latin languages. Jesus said to him, "Follow me." And he left everything, arose and followed Jesus.[20]

The gospels record Jesus dining with his disciples at Matthew's house. On hearing of this the Pharisees complained: "Why eateth your Master with publicans and sinners?" Jesus said: "They that be whole need not a physician but they that are sick."[21]

The first gospel is attributed to Matthew. It opens with the lineage of Jesus from Abraham and David. It was written for the benefit of the Jews, to prove to them that Jesus was indeed the Messiah that was prophesied. The illumination flame of the hierarchy of Gemini flows through this gospel. Some say Matthew suffered martyrdom; some say he died in peace.

James the Greater

James the Greater is on the six o'clock line, the sign of Cancer and the line of the Mother. He was a fisherman in Galilee with his father, Zebedee, and his brother, the apostle John. Jesus gave these brothers the name "Boanerges," meaning "sons of thunder," and evidently they were fiery personalities.

There is a tradition that after Jesus' ascension, James preached the gospel in Spain before returning to Jerusalem, where he was beheaded by Herod Agrippa in A.D. 44—making him the first of the apostles to face martyrdom. He is known as the apostle of Spain, and it is said that his body was miraculously transported there from Jerusalem following his death. His shrine at Santiago became one of the greatest pilgrimage centers in the Middle Ages. It is recorded that his last words were "Pax vobiscum," "Peace be with you," a benediction used by the Catholic Church to this day.

James later embodied as Clara Louise Kieninger, the first Mother of the Flame. She ascended on October 25, 1970, her soul being embodied in a feminine form in the victory of the six o'clock line of the Divine Mother.

Jude

Jude, who was also known as Lebbaeus or Judas Thaddeus, is on the seven o'clock line of the hierarchy of Leo. At the Last Supper he asked Jesus, "Lord, how is it that thou wilt manifest thyself unto us, and not unto the world?" Jesus answered, "If a man love me, he will keep my words: and my Father will love him, and we will come unto him, and make our abode with him."[22] In the Gospel accounts, this is the last question that any disciple asked Jesus before he prayed in Gethsemane.

The Causal Body of Jude holds the pattern of God-gratitude that overcomes hardness of heart and ingratitude in the world. The Epistle of Jude is attributed to him, and it is reported that he suffered martyrdom in Persia.

James the Less

James the Less is on the eight o'clock line under the sign of Virgo. It is said that James resembled Jesus so much in body and manner that it was difficult to distinguish one from the other, and that the kiss of Judas in the Garden of Gethsemane was necessary to make sure that Jesus and not James was taken prisoner.

He is often identified with James, the brother of Jesus, who is mentioned a number of times in Acts as a leader of the early Church in Jerusalem. Paul refers to Peter, James and John as "pillars" of the early Church, and James was the leader of the council convened to consider the question of the application of the Jewish law to gentile Christians.[23]

The period of James' leadership of the Church in Jerusalem was one of great persecution. James was esteemed for his purity and his self-mortification—he allowed his outer self to die and the Christ Self to manifest. He was called "the Just."

He was martyred in Jerusalem. Josephus gives the year as A.D. 62 and records that his death was by stoning, while the early Christian writer St. Hegesippus reports that he was thrown off the temple tower.

John the Beloved

John the Beloved is on the nine o'clock line, under the hierarchy of Libra. The gospel records that at the Last Supper he leaned upon the chest of Jesus and asked him who would betray him. Jesus said: "Him to whom I give the sop." He gave the sop to Judas, and John records that immediately Satan entered the heart of Judas to betray him.[24]

John was the only disciple who did not forsake Jesus as he was dying on the cross. As Jesus saw John standing nearby with Mary, he said to her, "Woman, behold thy son!" and said to John, "Behold thy Mother!"[25] Jesus thereby acknowledged John as his spiritual brother, as worthy to be the son of his own mother—and therefore, he elevated John to the level of Christ.

John embodied the full person of the Christ Self, and unless this had been true, Jesus would not have created that relationship, because Mary was Mother in the archetypal sense of Universal Mother—she embodied the Mother Flame. When Jesus called John her son, he was speaking not just in the physical sense but also in the universal sense of the Son of God, the Son of the Divine Mother, whose representative she was.

John stayed in Jerusalem for some time during the persecutions following Jesus' resurrection. After the martyrdom of Peter and Paul, John settled in Ephesus, the greatest city of Asia Minor, where Paul had centered his missionary activities. There is a tradition, which is confirmed by Tertullian and Jerome, that during the reign of Domitian, John was taken to Rome where an attempt to put him to death in a cauldron of boiling oil was miraculously thwarted. (This is the test of fire that was also faced by Shadrach, Meshach and Abednego.[26]) He emerged from the cauldron unharmed and was then banished to the island of Patmos. Here he received and recorded the Book of Revelation.

After the death of Domitian in the year A.D. 96, John could return to Ephesus, and many believe that he wrote his Gospel and three epistles at that time, when he was in his nineties.

Saint Jerome relates that "when he was earnestly pressed by the brethren to write his gospel, he answered he would do it, if by ordering a common fast they would all put up their prayers together to God."[27] John then received the revelation of the immortal first words of his gospel: "In the beginning was the Word."

John knew Jesus as the Christ and the Word, beyond the flesh-and-blood man. He never established Jesus as an idol, a flesh-and-blood Master to be worshiped; he saw him as the vehicle of the incarnation of the Word. Others have tried to make the person of Jesus the only vessel that God has ever used, thus circumscribing the eternal Word by the flesh-and-blood matrix in which he appeared for a mere thirty-three years.

John is said to have passed his last years at Ephesus, and to have died there at a great age, outliving all the other apostles. According to some, he simply "disappeared"—was translated like Elijah or "assumed" into heaven as was the Blessed Virgin. Others testify to the miracles wrought from the dust of his tomb.

Saint Jerome writes that in his final years at Ephesus, when he no longer had the strength to preach, he would ask to be carried to the assembly of the faithful and would say only these words: "My little children, love one another." When asked why he always repeated the same words, he replied, "Because it is the word of the Lord, and if you keep it you do enough."[28]

As an Ascended Master, John the Beloved has delivered a number of dictations through the Messengers, and our love for this apostle is boundless. When we hear his dictations, we feel the love that he continues to magnify to amplify Jesus' mission. It is a comfort to know that so great a being is holding that fire of victory that is the challenging of all treachery, intrigue, dishonesty—the perversions of the nine o'clock line. If you were born under the sign of Libra, then you are on that line with John, and you can call to his Causal Body to help you focus that flame of victory and the love that dissipates all the maya and illusion of the world.

Judas Iscariot

Judas Iscariot, the betrayer of Jesus, is on the ten o'clock line of Scorpio. He was the treasurer, the one who kept the funds for Jesus and the Apostles. The gospels record that he betrayed Jesus for thirty pieces of silver.

However, Judas realized his guilt and had great remorse; after the deed was done Satan left him and Judas could once again see clearly. Judas hanged himself; he could not stand the unreal self that he had espoused on the ten o'clock line, and he sought to destroy that self. However, his love for Jesus was great. He had such remorse that it propelled him into a life of total devotion in his next embodiment, which he spent in prayer and service. Because of his great devotion, he did win his ascension in that life.

Judas personified for us and showed us the great pitfall of failing the test of the ten. This is a test that comes to all. It is the temptation to forsake the cause for human comfort, human pleasure, human concern, selfishness and self-love. To fail that test is to betray the Christ in ourselves or in our fellowman. Each time we deny the Christ or allow the Christ to be desecrated by the world, we are betraying Jesus; we are betraying our own Christ consciousness.

The Book of Acts records that after Judas' betrayal, Matthias was chosen to replace him in the circle of the twelve: "And they appointed two, Joseph called Barsabas, who was surnamed Justus, and Matthias. And they prayed, and said, Thou, Lord, which knowest the hearts of all men, shew whether of these two thou hast chosen, that he may take part of this ministry and apostleship, from which Judas by transgression fell, that he might go to his own place. And they gave forth their lots; and the lot fell upon Matthias; and he was numbered with the eleven apostles."[29]

Simon

Simon is on the eleven o'clock line of Sagittarius. In the gospels he is surnamed "the Canaanite" or "Zelotes," both meaning "the Zealous."

He is said to have preached throughout Egypt, Britain, Armenia and Africa. According to some accounts he went to Britain with Joseph of Arimathea, and in others he preached with Jude in Persia, where they were both martyred.

FIGURE 7:
The Twelve Apostles on the Lines of the Clock

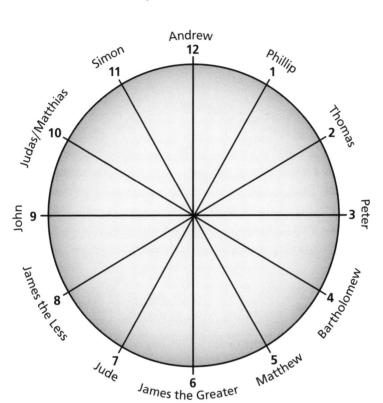

Individual Petals in a Mandala of Light

All that we are is the product of all who have gone before us, as we have been able to receive their imparting. We may all be students of Jesus, but we all may embody a different flame of the Master, a different quality, because we have all heard and seen and understood a little differently. Our perception is conditioned by our own attainment, our own personal geometric pattern, our own fragrance, our own understanding.

This is the individualization of the God Flame. This is how billions of lifewaves may each be the individuality of God and yet be different. And as they are spread throughout a cosmos like millions of stars or flowers, they would be arranged according to the gradations of the rainbow and the rays of God, according to the intensity of light, in a glorious pattern.

Looking at a sunflower, the many petals and the magnificent center, we realize that the hosts of the LORD form these formations, rhythmic patterns in movement, each of us a petal forming a grand design of a cosmic Causal Body. So we begin to realize the value of our individuality. If you were to take this great sunflower and begin to pluck its beautiful yellow petals, soon only the center would be left. Each petal is an identity, and if petal by petal they are taken, soon there is the loss of the mandala or the community or the Brotherhood of Light.

Recognizing the indissoluble oneness of the whole, recognizing the uniqueness of each part, recognizing that none can progress unless we do, we work very hard in our striving and our labor. We know every day the planetary consciousness will rise if we rise, and if we do not rise, it will remain the same. This is a perpetual understanding of the joy of service, the joy of the LORD, the joy of praying together, studying together and serving together. Building a community together is the realization of a patterned nucleus that will serve for the whole. What we dissolve in our members will serve for the whole; what we extol and uphold will be retained for the earth.

Christ, the Immaculate Concept "I Greet Thee, Lord"

Upon this rock I will build my church.

JESUS

# Christ, the Immaculate Concept "I Greet Thee, Lord"

I T IS ABSOLUTELY NECESSARY THAT EACH one who would rise into the true realization of brotherhood should salute the God in others, at the same time practicing the ritual of forgiveness, compassion and discrimination toward the outer manifestation. This means that the individual must strip himself of delusions concerning himself and others.

First of all, he must acknowledge the manifestation of the Divine Image in all parts of life by maintaining in his consciousness an immaculate or pure concept of the archetypal pattern of the Christ for every man, woman and child upon the planet. As one practices this ritual of beholding the Christ in all, he gains a momentum in the power of visualization that will evoke in others, where there is a responsive chord, the manifestation of the realities of cosmic identity.

Second, he should be entirely free from criticism, condemnation and judgment regarding what may be acting in the world of those with whom he is associated. If he has the gift of discernment of spirits,[1] he is, of course, more capable of understanding the difference between the Real Self, the human self and those benign or negative aspects that can play on the being of man.

Individuals can, at a given time, manifest an undesirable quality and then, at a later date, overcome or "come up over" their errors. Thus, it is folly for anyone who seeks true brotherhood to bind himself and others with limiting concepts. Give men the freedom to express as they will, but be on guard to recognize whether it is the outer or the inner man who is on stage at any given time.

The Covenant of Compassion

Lanello explains compassion as an aspect of true brotherhood: "The covenant of compassion is the key to victory. When you call for my mantle of victory in this year, O beloved, remember that it is won by the covenant of compassion. Those toward whom you are compassionate can be victorious because they know that you love them.

"Love someone today. Love someone each day with the kind of love for which the soul is yearning. For the world will offer its loves, but the soul remains hungry and weary and crying—crying out for the tenderness that understands it and does not merely take care of the creature comforts. When you give a meal or when you give physical aid, it is received in joy because the spirit that flows with it reaches the soul, and the soul is at peace and no longer under the strain of world distress....

"And where you see any son of light spearheading a cause, I say: Help him, encourage him, and offer that cup of light—not neglecting the cup of cold water, the food, the refreshment and the care. Providing physical needs is an essential part of the experience of love. Therefore, beloved hearts, recognize that when your bodies and minds have needs, these are supplied in the truest sense of love that need not be a descending spiral but one that uplifts and exalts and comforts by the eternal covenant of compassion."[2]

Compassion and loving-kindness, the bywords of the Bodhisattva, of necessity embody fearlessness. Saint Germain gives us his definition of fearless compassion: "I am Saint Germain. I, too, have spent the decades and centuries in the caves of the Himalayas and in the planes of nirvana. I come from a long preparation to embody the soul, the Law, the Flame, the ray that is called Aquarius....

"My emphasis as I tutor your souls is in the development of the heart as a fiery furnace and vortex of transmutation, a place where the threefold flame is balanced and where one can extend the borders of being and love to enfold so many who suffer.

"Think upon these words of the Bodhisattva vow, *fearless compassion!* Ah, what a state of mind to be in perpetually! Fearlessness to give of the fount of one's being, to extend compassion instead of criticism and backbiting, to give such flood tides of love as to fill in the chinks and cracks of another's shortcomings. Fearless compassion means one no longer fears to lose oneself or to loose oneself to become such a grid for the light to pass through that the Infinite One never ceases to be the compassionate one through you.

"Is this not, then, the face and the posture of the Buddha, our beloved Gautama? Is it not, beloved, that Presence of the Divine One?

"O fearlessness flame, dissolve, then, all reticence to be and to embrace the will to be! Fearlessness flame, sweep through those who are a part of my band of disciples and let each one know how the rings of the aura multiply as lines of compassion, even as rings upon a tree denote the ageless wisdom that accrues to one's Tree of Life—as a destiny, as a continuity of the extension of the branches of being until all of life might know that in the earth God has planted a seed and a seedling has come forth and a tree has matured: It has become a great tree. It is thyself, beloved, one and one and one again, trees of the forest of God where angels pray.

"Is it not so in order that the whole world might receive the extended branches of those who have fearless compassion? Let it be the byword of those who adore the kindling fire of Buddha of the heart."[3]

The Ritual of Forgiveness

For those who would espouse the path of the Bodhisattva, Saint Germain gives a profound teaching on the ritual of forgiveness and the danger of harboring resentment:

"In truth, when men understand the ritual of forgiveness and the ritual of honor, they will understand that as they reach out from their hearts to enfold one whom they meet with true and unbiased love, there flows from their hearts to that one an energy of upliftment that in contacting the receptive heart is raised exponentially into higher dimensions until, by the power of the square root, the cosmic cube glows within that energy and amplifies it by love. This positively charged energy then returns to the sender, assuring him that the blessings he will reap for the joy he has released to another will be a permanent part of his world forever....

"We urge, then, upon all an understanding of the ritual of the heart. When an individual does some bit of harm to you, precious ones, whether it be mischievous or intentional, you who are the wise ones will immediately seize upon the opportunity to forgive him.

"For when the essence of forgiveness is released from your

heart, not only does it create a passion for freedom in the erring one but it intensifies remorse in his heart, thereby bringing him to the feet of his own divinity. Thus, he is able once again to laugh at the wind and the wave and the seasons and the buffetings of life and understand that all is a chastening to unfold his soul's reality.

"Do you see, then, gracious ones, that courtesy as an expression of forgiveness and affection between hearts is a spiritual activity that brings about great soul expansion, which is intended to bring every man from serfdom to a state of lordship where he is the master of his world?

"Yet we sometimes look askance, even from our octave, at those individuals who have long been under our tutelage and our radiation who upon receipt of some trivial offense, immediately begin to send out a vibration of great resentment against the one who performs this offense against their lifestreams.

"Quite frequently there is a mounting of intense reactionary resentment; this creates a great karma for the student of Ascended Master law, who ought to know better. And through the rupture that is thereby created in the emotional body, there is a pressing in from the sinister force of disturbing vibrations that not only flow through the aura and lifestream of the one who has taken offense but also puncture the peace and harmony of the supposed offender.

"Do you not see, then, by contrast what a gracious thing the ritual of forgiveness can be? And oh how wonderful it would be if our students would truly understand the law of forgiveness! It is a sweet gift from the heart of God and one that people ought to welcome into their worlds so that they may freely give it to others, even as they have freely received it.

"Whenever someone does something that is not to your liking, precious ones, this is your great opportunity. This is your opportunity to say, 'I will use God's energy and love to erase one more blight upon the universe! I will see to it that the blackboard of life becomes a radiant screen of white perfection, and I will put my perfection-patterns into manifestation. For these patterns are from the Father, and I am the Son representing the Father and I must show forth Light and not Darkness.'

"Don't you think it a bit strange, gracious ones, that from time to time people insist upon doing just the opposite? With their mouths they attempt to draw near to God as they speak and prattle of brotherly love; but when the moment of testing comes, they are the first ones to rise up and say, 'Vengeance is mine!' What a mockery this makes of 'pure religion and undefiled before God and the Father.'[4]

"Let us, then, seek not after lust or luster but let us seek after the perfectionment of life. The perfectionment of life lives within you. It is quite natural to draw light from within your heart and send it out into the world. This is the virtue that creates the seamless garment. Do you realize that your tube of light is the seamless garment of the Christ? Do you realize when you call forth from God the perfection of his light-radiance to surround you that you are weaving the seamless garment around yourself?

"Precious ones, I want you all to understand tonight that the moment that you have in your thought and feeling world resentment against any individual or any group of individuals on earth, you are immediately sending forth through the qualification of your energy the substance that will create a boomerang that will bring to your doorstep a great deal of unhappiness.

"You do not wish to reap the fruit of unhappiness, do you? Then I am certain you will understand that even if you do not always feel like forgiving, it is that discretion which is the better part, in fact the best part, of valor."[5]

The Path of Loving-Kindness

Lord Maitreya tells us how the challenge to embody the virtue of loving-kindness motivated him on the Path: "I come to initiate the line of Bodhisattvas of the New Age. I come to inquire: Are there any among you who care enough for Terra to live and to love, and to live and to serve until this people, held in the hand of God, come into the center of the One? . . .

"Here I AM, and startling as it may seem, I have always been with you, even in the darkest hours of your aloneness, even in the hour of your rejection of my presence when you have cried out, 'Whither shall I flee from thy presence?' For you have known in your soul that although you would ascend into heaven or be in the depths of the underworld,[6] you would find Maitreya Buddha answering the call of Gautama Buddha, of Sanat Kumara."[7]

Lord Maitreya encourages his chelas to cultivate the quality of loving-kindness: "One tender smile is surely worth a thousand frames of the face of Maitreya. The loving, overflowing, pure heart's giving—does this not convey the Maitreya beyond the veil? I desire you to be myself, not in pomposity or pride (now self-styled initiators of lesser mortals), nay, but to remember that by the grace of the one who has sent me, you yourself might be my vessel.

"You say, then, 'But you have not yet appeared to us, Maitreya. How can we be thyself appearing to others?'

"Yet I have so many times appeared to you. . . .

"You shall surely know the Buddha in the way when you expand the golden pink glow-ray of the heart, becoming thereby tender, sensitive, loving in a beautiful sound of love—love as appreciation for the soul, for the spirit, for the vastness of potential and being, but above all love as appreciation for the God Flame.

"In gratitude for the God Flame that is your threefold flame, serve to set life free. Kindness always comes forth from gratitude. Selfishness emits from the state of the ingrate who receives again and again and demands more and demands more again as though life and Hierarchy and Mother should supply all wants and needs.

"Blessed ones, to forget to be grateful for the gift of the Flame of Life means that you can be capable of riding rough-shod over another's tenderest moments and feelings in this insensitivity.

"The Keeper's Daily Prayer is given to you by the beloved Nada that you might neglect not profoundest gratitude in the daily memory that you are and shall be eternally yourself because the Flame of Life as divine spark beats—beats, beloved—and leaps, burns and blazes within you. All else may fade, but the flame burns on, and out of the flame is heard the Call, the Call to the soul:

"'Come Home to the heart of Maitreya!'"[8]

In profound gratitude for the gift of the Flame of Life whereby we extend kindness and fearless compassion to all life, let us offer "The Keeper's Daily Prayer" to the Buddhas and Bodhisattvas who have carved the Path before us.

The Keeper's Daily Prayer
by Lady Master Nada

A flame is active—
A flame is vital—
A flame is eternal.

I AM a God Flame of radiant love
From the very heart of God
In the Great Central Sun,

Descending from the Master of Life!
I AM charged now
With beloved Helios and Vesta's
Supreme God consciousness
And solar awareness.

Pilgrim upon earth,
I AM walking daily the way
Of the Ascended Masters' victory
That leads to my eternal freedom
By the power of the sacred fire
This day and always,
Continually made manifest
In my thoughts, feelings and immediate awareness,
Transcending and transmuting
All the elements of earth
Within my four lower bodies
And freeing me by the power of the sacred fire
From those misqualified foci of energy within my being.

I AM set free right now from all that binds
By and through the currents of the Divine Flame
Of the sacred fire itself,
Whose ascending action makes me
God in manifestation,
God in action,
God by direction and
God in consciousness!

I AM an active flame!
I AM a vital flame!
I AM an eternal flame!
I AM an expanding fire spark
From the Great Central Sun
Drawing to me now every ray

Of divine energy which I need
And which can never be requalified by the human
And flooding me with the light
And God-illumination of a thousand suns
To take dominion and rule supreme forever
Everywhere I AM!

Where I AM, there God is also.
Unseparated forever I remain,
Increasing my light
By the smile of his radiance,
The fullness of his love,
The omniscience of his wisdom,
And the power of his life eternal,
Which automatically raises me
On ascension's wings of victory
That shall return me to the heart of God
From whence in truth
I AM come to do God's will
And manifest abundant life to all!

Compassion and Forgiveness

Maitreya has been called the "Compassionate One." The name *Maitreya* itself is derived from the Sanskrit word *maitri*, meaning "kindness" or "love." Maitreya exemplifies the Bodhisattva's virtues of kindness, fearless compassion and *virya*, or vigor.*

And in order to be charitable or forgiving, you need *virya*. If you don't have strength, you have nothing to give—you don't

---

*In Buddhist teachings *virya* is one of the ten *paramitas* ("perfect virtues" or "highest perfections") that one must practice and perfect as a prerequisite to the attainment of Bodhisattvahood. *Virya* has been translated as "strength," "energy," "strenuousness," "manliness," "zeal," "courage," "power," "diligence," or "vigor."

even have the energy to forgive. It takes strength to fulfill your own needs and then have something left over to give to others.

Thus, Maitreya speaks not only of compassion but also of mercy and forgiveness: "I come to fill your hearts with mercy and compassion, with the pink and the violet of the amethyst egg with ascension's flame anchored therein.[9]

"I would touch your hearts through the Mother that they might be filled to overflowing with the balm of mercy and compassion so needed by the world in the coming year and always and so needed by you as you move among mankind, dispensing the light of God.

"In order to enter the Path, souls need forgiveness and love. By extending the love and the forgiveness of God, you prepare the way for their acceptance of our offering as teaching, as initiation. Always remember that love must be without dissimulation; it must be given freely, abundantly, equally, to all who come to you for assistance.

"When you have given love and more love, extend also mercy. As the flame of forgiveness becomes the adornment of the soul praying in the temple—the robe of the devotee, the shawl of the humble—so is mercy a garment to be worn, signifying the atonement of the Mediator, the intercession of the Mother and the dispensations of Hierarchy.

"I come, then, to the place where mankind are found in life, needing to be washed clean, needing the flow of the waters of the Word, needing to know that they are loved in compassion and compassion's flame....

"I have come, as I have told you, with a very special increment of light for your heart. It is a soothing action and a mellowing action. Where some of you have records of hardness of heart, a softening can take place if you will, a tenderness, filling your heart with such mercy as to make you more supple to the flow of love to all mankind.

"You know that I am a master of the crown chakra and of Wisdom's flame. Then understand that I deem it important to clear the way in the heart for the coming of the light of the crown that you should be found to be the most merciful and most compassionate of people.

"This does not mean that you allow souls to indulge their human consciousness. The very foundation of mercy and compassion is the grid of the will of God; it is the outline that is firm. In the firmness of that chalice, love and mercy can flow yet not be compromised by those who would flaunt the Law.

"Let the eye of the sons and daughters of God release a tender regard for all life, and behind the tender regard let there be the piercing brilliance of the will of God, of the eye of Morya. Do you not understand that to gaze into Serapis' eye is to see disciplined love?

The Return to Eden

"Many times, although the outer man rebels, the inner soul is so grateful to receive love in the form of a discipline that will propel the soul into the likeness of its Maker. Love and mercy take many forms. To cast out the twin flames from the circle of oneness called the Garden of Eden was a supreme act of mercy and compassion and yet was the sternness of the Law.

"Rather than allow them to pass through the second death for their sins, the LORD God provided the opportunity for their return to Paradise lost. What if that opportunity was toiling by the sweat of the brow, pain and the experience of outer darkness? Is this not calculated, by the most intense ray of compassion, to propel souls back to the center of that garden of wisdom?

"The Edenic consciousness is the goal of your life. You are living on a planetary home sustained by love and mercy to give you the opportunity to return through the open door of

Christ consciousness to the white-fire core, to the Tree of Life and to the tree of the knowledge of good and evil, where your immaculate conception of absolute perfection will be restored.

"Going back to the Garden of Eden is a step-by-step process of initiation—each erg of energy spilled upon the ground must be recaptured in love. You are coming nearer and nearer to Edenic bliss as you worship the I AM Presence, as you see that Presence as the Tree of Life. As you sit under that tree and meditate in the Christ Self and in the Flame, you are surrounded by cherubim keeping the way of the Tree of Life. The guardian action of the angelic hosts is the action of the Flame, the action of mercy and of compassion.

"I AM that light which lighteth every man and woman that cometh into the world.[10] I AM the light of the Holy of holies, and I would transfer that light to you, the portion for your return.

"Mankind has thought that the concept of the Fall was mere allegory. How can they think this when their souls hold the memory of Paradise lost? How can they think this when they see themselves aged, decrepit, subject to disease, incomplete, burdened by karma and unhappiness?

"Surely God did not will these conditions. Surely all who are fair toward God and self must recognize that individual responsibility is the only factor in present circumstances and conditions. This is the responsible teaching. This is the action of the Great Central Sun Magnet. This is compassion. Unless these conditions come upon mankind to teach them the error of their ways, how can they learn that fire is hot, that ice is cold? How can they learn the thousand-and-one facts about cause-and-effect sequences? How can they learn?

"Karma is not punishment; karma is mercy and compassion that would preserve the soul in eternity, that would draw the soul back to God and therefore, that must teach the soul the way of Christ-mastery.

"I am initiating you in love that love might become the magnet of your God-desire—God in you desiring to be whole, God in you desiring to be the fullness of Christ peace, God in you desiring to be perfection in the Law. I AM the fullness of love that is the fulfillment of every need, human and divine.

"I would make of you as quickly as possible true initiates on the Path, true disciples of the Christ and the Buddha. I would make you as quickly as possible the authority for your life and for your world. I would make you teachers of the children of God. I would make you instruments for the passing of the fires of regeneration.

"I send forth the light of the resurrection flame! I send forth the light of the will of God! Now, if you would become all these things that I would have you become, you must accept the chastening fire, the intensification of the fire and the accompanying discomfort as your atoms and molecules adjust to the fervent heat of God's love."[11]

Maitreya sums up his teachings on the development of the heart in loving-kindness: "Know me, then, in kindness first expressed by you. Then the return current of that kindness expressed by another will reveal to you one of my million smiles through the friend, through the kind ones on earth, the wise ones who know that true kindness is found in the act of one who has cared enough to earn the key to open the door to successive chambers of my retreat.

"Come and find me, beloved."[12]

The Caravan of God

Jesus says: "You are children of one father, our Father universal. The bounties of his heart at times fly away from man's consciousness because he insists upon filling his mind with the banalities of reason, those futile efforts that are of the dark, of separation and vanity. As the preacher said long ago, 'Vanity of vanities, all is vanity.'[13] When mankind understand the vanity of their lives as the fruitlessness thereof, they will perceive that that which they have felt to be fruit in many cases denied me before men.

"All are my children as they are God's children, for we have one Father, and the light of hope shines through a realization of the content of his mind, of his compassion, of his feelings for ye all.

"You are not given up. There is hope wherever there is life and wherever that life responds to the vibratory action that clearly has said, Come let us reason together, saith the Lord: though your sins be as scarlet, I will make them white as snow.[14] The effulgence of my love is the cup of God and his mercy, drops of life overflowing into the void of mankind's unknowing, and flooding mankind with the certainty of knowing.

"What is the meaning of compassion and grace and understanding? Are these things now so far removed from you that you are unable to understand these things, not as the dregs of human sympathies drooling in the cup and mocking the very Great Giver himself, but rather as the compassion of the universal caravan coming down from the moments of the beginning to this hour and proceeding in its orderly fashion across the deserts of life to those tender places preserved by God within each individual life as the opportunity to hold dear and near elements of compassion and grace, not only for others but also for yourselves, not only for yourselves but also for others. For in the great balance of the outgoing of the cosmic nature of man, he is resurrected. He resurrects within himself the plan.

"The streams from out the Central Sun, these are light for everyone. The communion cup I hold in hand is heaven's own law that now makes demand upon the universe. Will ye drink of the cup which I have drunk of? Will ye be endowed with the grace which I am endowed with? Will you understand the meaning of the outflow of compassion? Forgiveness to all, yea, for all have erred. Restoration to all, for all have shared the joy of the Archangels....

"I AM come to fulfill the Law. I AM come to fulfill the law of your life. I AM come within each of ye to produce the miracle of cosmic abundance. I AM come that all men might have life and that abundantly.[15] I AM come that there might be a great clapping and stirring of the hearts of men, angels and elementals. I AM come that all nature might be endowed with a sense of universal abundance and no lack....

"[Mankind] have failed in their understanding to apprehend the caravan of God. But I tell unto you, this day, the great fact that the caravan of God has moved across the deserts, and with the caravan of God, he also has gone. God is with the caravan. He may appear in the tiny shepherd child. He may appear in the foreign face. He may appear in the unexpected place. It does not matter, for God has appeared and God is and he walks among men....

"Let me tell you this, that the highest manifestation of God walks also in the Christ of every man, and man should understand this, for those who love me as I AM will understand the great love of the I AM Presence within them.

"They will understand that in this love there is a compassion for all ages, not only the caravan of today and the caravan of yesterday, but the caravan of tomorrow and all of the tomorrows and the foreverness of God which are captivated together in one giant cup of universal light, the intelligence of the ages compounding, then, its wisdom rays to all mankind and fashioning those instruments of deliverance that will bring to the ages the kingdom of heaven, the kingdom of beauty, the kingdom of perfection and the kingdom of strength. And as the sun shineth in his strength, so also shall the rays of this king-dom penetrate to all parts of the earth."[16]

The Dangers of Criticism

Morya gives a report on the dangers of criticism, condemnation and judgment of others: "Throughout the years, beloved Saint Germain and others of the holy band composing our council have continued to admonish the students of the many activities linked with the Great White Brotherhood or attached, at least, to the ideals of that Brotherhood. These admonishments have taken many forms such as exhortation, pin-pointing, phrasing and rephrasing of little-known laws, subtle expositions of the fine points of esoteric instructions and generally specific advice....

"Men can only harm themselves or project harm at another life; they can never damage the invulnerable Deity. However, as the Christ declared and as we reaffirm: 'Whatever is done to the least of the children of the light is an act done to the Holy Christ Self of that one whose face ever beholds the face of his own mighty I AM Presence.' ('Inasmuch as ye have done it unto one of the least of these my brethren, ye have done it unto me.... Take heed that ye despise not one of these little ones; for I say unto you, That in heaven their angels do always behold the face of my Father which is in heaven.'[17])

"Any harmful act is referred to the Holy Christ Self and becomes a part of the life record of the person who commits it, and it must one day be balanced before the Lords of Karma. Whether mankind, in their human concepts, like this idea—whether it appeals to them or not—the fact remains that it is pure Truth, and I AM determined to declare it as a protection to those who observe its precepts.

"Ever so frequently, conceited individuals, who count

themselves exceedingly wise, determine that they shall criticize or judge another. They do this although fully aware of the scriptures, which clearly state the Great Law, 'Judge not, that ye be not judged. For with what judgment ye judge, ye shall be judged: and with what measure ye mete, it shall be measured to you again.'[18]...Such acts always travel the full circle back to the very door of the one sending them out....

"In this report I wish to emphasize and clarify certain not generally known aspects of the effects of criticism. When applied by human reason or observation to another, without being voiced, it is mildly destructive. But when it is uttered aloud to another, it is amplified at least ten times. En route to the one criticized, it gathers more of the elements of the mass mind's condemnation, until it is an arrow both sharp and swift, finding easy penetration into the tender mind of the one to whom it is directed—unless that one is extremely alert.

"When released by a friend or relative to whom the individual is receptive, it often lodges within their subconsciousness to perform its work of destruction as an arrow of pestilence—silent, invisible, insidious. It is not the weight of the minor criticism, sometimes charged in innocence, that counts; it is the mounting momentum of the mass consciousness, using the thoughtform created by the one sitting in the seat of the scornful, which makes criticism deadly. It is for this reason that beloved Saint Germain has articulated so frequently against such conduct. This is why he so fervently decries it.

"When penetration occurs within the psyche of a lifestream, the healing arts of spiritual love and the golden oil of peace are needed. For of a truth, the individual becomes the victim of a robber band and needs the ministrations of the Good Samaritan. Countless men and women of world stature have been hindered in their missions, and some have been completely diverted from their life plan by the deliberate or thoughtless acts of others through criticism. Some of these, when lying as helpless victims of this form of destructivity, have been ignored by the righteous who murmur, 'They must have deserved this. It must have been their karma.'

"I stress two points of great import to the student who would successfully avert such calamity and calumny. Firstly, avoid participation in judgment and condemnation in any measure. Secondly, be Good Samaritans to those who are the victims of this human cruelty. By carrying out these two services, you will become, in effect, participants in the tenets of the Order of Samaria (the Good Samaritans), of which I have been master for centuries. You will also be doing the will of God and ensuring the protection of the light to your own lifestream."[19]

The Faculty of Discrimination

The faculty of discrimination is the balance, or razor's edge, of consciousness. It is the yardstick of perfection that, when rightly employed, can bring about spiritual progress in oneself and in others; when wrongly used, it is a burden to the soul. Discrimination is the ability to recognize the need for improvement in all, to help another through a difficult situation without allowing oneself to become emotionally involved in or disturbed by the situation and without giving the power of Reality to the discordant manifestation. Discrimination is being aware of the clouds and knowing that the sun is just behind them.

In considering the bearing of another, it is unwise to take one minor point or even a major one as representative of that one's norm of expression. It is well not to be hasty in assessing the character of another. Assemble facts, if you must, and gradually arrive at an estimate of what appears to be the pattern of a person's life—always bearing in mind the standard of perfection held in the heart of each one's Christ Self on behalf of the soul that is in a state of becoming.

Nevertheless, when it is necessary to make a decision about your associates, trust your first impression, pray and follow the intuitive promptings of your heart. Be practical in dealing with the human consciousness, realizing its present limitations while recognizing that at any moment it might leap into the matrix of its divine identity. Do not be unduly harsh or unduly lenient, for strong feelings lead to sympathetic attractions or repulsions that can create no bond of real brotherhood.

Religion: The Binding Power of Brotherhood

Religion is intended to bind the individual to God and to his fellowman.* But there are abroad in the world today many misconceptions and wrong attitudes that divide mankind and have resulted in people turning away from the religious life.

Millions upon earth seek no more than the comforts of a material existence, material wealth and material happiness, often ignoring the beckonings of their own great spiritual identity. Yet their masterful I AM Presence would gladly inform them of the truths of life concerning their reason for being. The Presence would teach them all things that it might raise them in the spiritual peerage from the serfdom of self-indulgence to the kingdom of the Divine Image from on high. This image manifests upon the earth below in the birth of the Christ consciousness in every man, woman and child.

Those who have the Christ consciousness will have the true sense of brotherhood. They will understand that they have been born to serve. They will understand the precept of the Masters: "He that would be great among you, let him be the servant of all."[20] Christ the King is then crowned in every man who will accept the universality of his consciousness.

---

*The word *religion* is derived from the Latin *religio,* "bond between man and the gods," or *religare,* "to bind back."

Serapis Bey teaches the importance of a spirit of unity and cooperation in spiritual organizations: "To a Christian who says he does not need to belong to a church to be a follower of Christ, we would say, 'Quite true.' But we would shed light upon the subject.

"We have had some experience in these matters. We have found that those who cannot or are not willing to harmonize themselves enough to live in a spirit of cooperation and service with their fellowmen in a constructive spiritual organization— especially one which we sponsor—are usually far from being ready, as they may think they are, to follow the Christ or to receive our deeper teachings and assistance. For the most part they need to be left alone by us for quite some time, and this we often do as the best discipline for their natures.

"Bear in mind that although their tenets may differ, the purposes of all faiths are quite similar. While the ultimate faith may yet be sought, I am certain that in unity for the light, there is strength. And therein is to be found the fruit of that cooperative endeavor that is never realized in going it alone or in expressing continual disapproval of this or that phase of the outer organization or of the outer personalities of its leaders. Those religious structures whose purposes are both high and holy and that originated in our own consciousness should not be condemned for flaws, which the expanding Christ consciousness of its members will surely bypass unto victory.

"One of the functions of spiritual fraternities such as the Keepers of the Flame is the training of disciples to overcome personal differences and antipathies through loving associations dedicated to service. It is through active participation in spiritually constructive organizations that testing makes possible the disciple's learning the art of true love. For therein he learns to continue even when in difficulty to be wholly constructive toward God and man, offering gratitude to the Almighty in genuine happiness for the blessed opportunity of showing his loyalty to him by being loyal to a truly worthy cause."[21]

The Purpose of the Church

We understand ourselves a part of the body of God in heaven and the body of God on earth, and we count ourselves one with every other part of God—whether Jew or Christian or Moslem, Hindu, Buddhist, Zoroastrian, or Confucian, or none of these. Whether you have a religion or you do not have a religion, we recognize ourselves as one with the essential light in all people; we see no barriers of doctrine or dogma in any faith because it is the one stream of consciousness out of which we are born. The terminology may differ, the signs may differ, the language, but it is still the one Spirit, the one Christ, the one I AM Presence.

We understand that in this age of Aquarius, the coming of the Holy Spirit designates the Church as the community. When Jesus stated that he was founding his church ("Upon this rock I will build my church."[22]), the word in the original Greek is *ekklesia*, meaning "community of the called-out ones." It is not an institution, not the confines of doctrine and dogma or a building—it is the temple built without hands. And the sign of the members of that church, that Church Universal and Triumphant of Jesus Christ, is the sign of the white stone that is given in the Book of Revelation to those who overcome, to those who endure.[23] These also receive the new name that no man knoweth save the Father, the name that is the inner key of identity.

We all need that key of identity, and we are all marked by the inner light. And so the temple made without hands manifests within our very midst as a community, as an energy, as a love, as a oneness and a sense of ourselves together in the Holy Spirit as one person, one body, soul and heart—one in this living flame of eternal life.

Hilarion speaks of the purpose of the Church as this community of the Lightbearers: "The purpose of Church ... is for Lightbearers to be called out from society to keep the pillars of faith and of hope and of charity. The Church is the place where souls can ascend to a higher plane of communion because priest or priestess at the altar does keep a Flame that does become a magnet whereby the soul can rise week upon week back to her Source.

"The Church must elevate. It must not degrade. It must not seek popularity and to move to the level of the descent of the light in the populace. Let there then be an understanding that the Church has always been the avenue for the soul to reach out for holiness, to be sanctified, to receive the Body and Blood of our Lord. The Church is the open door whereby those who would may move toward sainthood.

"Let it be understood that there are many secular institutions, that there are many places for social activity, but the Church has come down from the traditions of the ancient temples of God where a living flame did burn upon the altar, where the flame was tended by devotions, by hymns and prayers and mantras, sustaining, then, upon its altar in this physical octave some portion of the Spirit above."[24]

The State of the Church Today

The Ascended Master Pope John XXIII comes with a serious report on the condition of the Church today: "I come to report to this body and to the earth that the hierarchies of heaven have seen that those who have entered the Church of the Lord who have compromised doctrine, who have set forth tenets of fear and of ignorance, who have compromised the communion, the Laws of God and the honor of God, constitute a cancer growing and infesting within the Church that was founded by our Lord and that has persisted in one form or another unto this time.

"There is need upon earth for the white stone,[25] the white cube that is the foundation stone, that is the Christ, the chief cornerstone of all building.[26] That white stone can be composed only of those souls who have united with the Spirit of God, with the I AM Presence, through that blessed Mediator, the Christ in all. There cannot be, then, the true Church, the one Church, so long as any portion of its members are in a consciousness of compromise, dishonor, or betrayal of the true teachings of our Lord.

"Ecumenism has failed because it has entered into compromise. There is no area of compromise! The teachings of the Christ represent a hurdle over which the carnal mind cannot pass. It must first surrender and make way for the Christ. We cannot, then, condone the action of the lowering of the hurdle to the level where the carnal mind and all of the animals of the barnyard of the electronic belt can hop over into the holy place. This is that abomination of desolation standing in the holy place where it ought not.[27]

"You see, then, when compromise holds sway, purity is not preserved—not for the elect, not for the children of God, not for the fallen ones. And then the Church crumbles, becomes dead ritual—a hollow echo of former things, former glory and the hope that was, that cannot be realized because the honor flame has fallen to the ground. . . .

"So I have come forth in the order of hierarchy to stand before you, that you might receive the momentum of our light and our love; for we are for the light of the Ancient of Days,[28] of Sanat Kumara. We are for the light of the earth! We are for the light of the Christ! And only if there be established a body of God upon earth who will not compromise this our devotion, this our energy, can we continue to serve the planet Earth."[29]

El Morya, who was Thomas More in one of his embodiments, has been a stalwart champion for the Church for centuries. He warns:

"Thus we see that the fallen ones desire the dispersion of light both to weaken and neutralize the Lightbearers and to give it unto their own masses, whom they use in wars, political elections, revolutions, riots and movements of various sorts that they might have the light to further the causes of the rivalrous Nephilim.

"Therefore, you will hear people be for this and for that. 'I am for a one-world religion,' they will say. But you must ask, 'What kind of world religion? Under whose domination? A World Council of Churches that denies the individualization of the God Flame? That denies the divinity of Christ in every man? That denies the option for the resurrection and the ascension? That denies karma and reincarnation as a cycle and a spiral of opportunity and a path of initiation?'

"The more centralized is control, the less control the individual may exercise over his own life. Whether in religion or a universal academy of science or medicine or the government, you will see that unless it is truly God who is at the center of their sun, there can only be the red sun going down that is not of the light....

"Therefore, understand the meaning of the term *universal*. The Universal Christ, the universal doctrine, the universal Godgovernment is a thing that exists in itself. It is that something that is present and real as the etheric matrix, as the garment of every lightbearer, as the light upon the altar of the heart. Up to this hour, that universality cannot be outpictured; for by definition, the moment that etheric matrix hits time and space and begins to come into form, immediately it is boxed; and there is the contriving and then there is the arguing and then the wars accelerating for who shall have the seat of power, who shall bear the sign of authority.

"Blessed ones of the Sun, the Church Universal is the Church Triumphant. It exists in the etheric octave and in those in embodiment who are the devotees who have daily contact with that etheric octave in the inner temples with the Ascended Masters, with the hosts of the light—who have killed ambition and pride, who have killed their desire to be thought great and powerful and to be preferred, who have killed their flesh-and-blood definitions of self and other selves, who have put to rest all desire to acquire anything but God, God and more God.

"These are the ones who remain in the earth, pillars of fire. 'Pillars of eternity,' I have called you.[30] For your roots are in the earth, your branches are in heaven, you remain the strong trees of life who do not allow the planet to become barren for the withdrawal of the universal matrix."[31]

The Brotherhood of Man

Let us conclude with El Morya's vision of the brotherhood of man under the Fatherhood of God: "The truly wise leave all judgment to God and pursue brotherhood as a spiritual ideal, ever holding the concept of discipleship and the ascension into perfection, while keeping the door to true brotherhood open.

"Such as these compassionately recognize all men as climbing step-by-step the rungs of the ladder of attainment. And although they may dwell temporarily upon the different heights to which they have attained, the wise foretell the day of their ultimate victory above the stages and steps of all human concepts and hold for their brother-pilgrims the immaculate concept of perfect Christ-discrimination.

"The brotherhood of man, when under the Fatherhood of

God, is a true Rock of Gibraltar to the planet Earth. All that betrays this brotherhood is each man's own betrayer; all that aids this brotherhood is cooperative love for the Saviour of the world.

" 'Lord, when saw we thee an hungered, and fed thee? Or thirsty, and gave thee drink? When saw we thee a stranger, and took thee in? Or naked, and clothed thee? Or when saw we thee sick, or in prison, and came unto thee? . . .

" 'Verily, I say unto you, Inasmuch as ye have done it unto one of the least of these my brethren, ye have done it unto me.' "[32]

Brotherhood Is Hierarchy in the Making

Brotherhood as a manifestation of the Holy Spirit is the cohesive power of the atom.

The body of God is, in reality, one.

The universe is one.

The galaxy is one.

The solar system is one.

The planet is one.

Man is one.

Anything inflicted upon any part of the body of God must manifest on the self.

Everyone is destined to fill a position in hierarchy; therefore brotherhood is hierarchy in the making. Brotherhood is the structure set up by the Hierarchy for the initiations of ascended man, and when passed, these initiations enable individuals to become a part of the Great White Brotherhood. When true brotherhood manifests on earth then, the hierarchical pattern will be seen here and now. Brotherhood is the blessed tie that binds the Hierarchy together.

Prayer for Brotherhood

Out of the One,
Thou, God, hast spun
All of the races of men.
By thy great Law
Do thou now draw
All to their God source again.

Take away hate;
By love abate
All mankind's vicious intent.
Show thy great pow'r
Every hour
Of love and compassion God sent.

I AM, I AM, I AM
Divine love sending forth
The wonderful feeling of true divine healing,
Unguents of light now sealing
All of the schisms of men.

Stop all division!
By God-precision
Love is the hallowed law-key.
Ultimate peace,
Make all war cease,
Let the children of men now go free!

Stop mankind's friction,
All their predictions
Tearing bless'd heart from heart.
By God-direction
Produce now perfection
In thy great family—one heart.

The Chart of Your Divine Self

THE CHART OF YOUR DIVINE SELF IS a portrait of you and of the God within you. It is a diagram of you and your potential to become who you really are. It is an outline of your spiritual anatomy.

The upper figure is your "I AM Presence," the Presence of God that is individualized in each one of us. It is your personalized "I AM THAT I AM." Your I AM Presence is surrounded by seven concentric spheres of spiritual energy that make up what is called your "Causal Body." The spheres of pulsating energy contain the record of the good works you have performed since your very first incarnation on earth. They are like your cosmic bank account.

The middle figure in the chart represents the "Holy Christ Self," who is also called the Higher Self. You can think of your Holy Christ Self as your chief guardian angel and dearest friend, your inner teacher and voice of conscience. Just as the I AM Presence is the presence of God that is individualized for each of us, so the Holy Christ Self is the presence of the

Universal Christ that is individualized for each of us. "The Christ" is actually a title given to those who have attained oneness with their Higher Self, or Christ Self. That is why Jesus was called "Jesus, the Christ."

What the Chart shows is that each of us has a Higher Self, or "Inner Christ," and that each of us is destined to become one with that Higher Self—whether we call it the Christ, the Buddha, the Tao or the Atman. This "Inner Christ" is what the Christian mystics sometimes refer to as the "inner man of the heart," and what the Upanishads mysteriously describe as a being the "size of a thumb" who "dwells deep within the heart."

We all have moments when we feel that connection with our Higher Self—when we are creative, loving, joyful. But there are other moments when we feel out of sync with our Higher Self—moments when we become angry, depressed, lost. What the spiritual path is all about is learning to sustain the connection to the higher part of ourselves so that we can make our greatest contribution to humanity.

The shaft of white light descending from the I AM Presence through the Holy Christ Self to the lower figure in the Chart is the crystal cord (sometimes called the silver cord). It is the "umbilical cord," the lifeline, that ties you to Spirit.

Your crystal cord also nourishes that special, radiant Flame of God that is ensconced in the secret chamber of your heart. It is called the threefold flame, or divine spark, because it is literally a spark of sacred fire that God has transmitted from his heart to yours. This flame is called "threefold" because it engenders the primary attributes of Spirit—power, wisdom and love.

The mystics of the world's religions have contacted the divine spark, describing it as the seed of divinity within. Buddhists, for instance, speak of the "germ of Buddhahood" that exists in every living being. In the Hindu tradition, the Katha Upanishad speaks of the "light of the Spirit" that is concealed in the "secret high place of the heart" of all beings.

Likewise, the fourteenth-century Christian theologian and mystic Meister Eckhart teaches of the divine spark when he says, "God's seed is within us."

When we decree, we meditate on the flame in the secret chamber of our heart. This secret chamber is your own private meditation room, your interior castle, as Teresa of Avila called it. In Hindu tradition, the devotee visualizes a jeweled island in his heart. There he sees himself before a beautiful altar, where he worships his teacher in deep meditation.

Jesus spoke of entering the secret chamber of the heart when he said: "When thou prayest, enter into thy closet, and when thou hast shut thy door, pray to thy Father which is in secret; and thy Father which seeth in secret shall reward thee openly."

The lower figure in the Chart of Your Divine Self represents you on the spiritual path, surrounded by the violet flame and the protective white light of God. The soul is the living potential of God—the part of you that is mortal but that can become immortal.

The purpose of your soul's evolution on earth is to grow in self-mastery, balance your karma and fulfill your mission on earth so that you can return to the spiritual dimensions that are your real home. When your soul at last takes flight and ascends back to God and the heaven-world, you will become an Ascended Master, free from the rounds of karma and rebirth. The high-frequency energy of the violet flame can help you reach that goal more quickly.

The Chart of Your Divine Self

Notes

Introduction

1. Gen. 2:9.

Section I • "I and My Father Are One"

Opening quotation: El Morya, *Pearls of Wisdom,* vol. 6, no. 7, February 15, 1963.

1. Lanto, April 8, 1971.
2. El Morya, "The Trek Upward Is Worth the Inconvenience!" *Keepers of the Flame Lesson 3.*
3. El Morya, *Pearls of Wisdom,* vol. 6, no. 8, February 22, 1963.

Section II • Expressions of Individuality

Opening quotation: Acts 17:26.

1. Luke 10:30–37.
2. The seven rays are the light emanations of the Godhead that emerge from the white light through the prism of the Christ consciousness. The seven rays are (1) blue, (2) yellow, (3) pink, (4) white, (5) green, (6) purple and gold, and (7) violet.
3. Matt. 6:27; 10:30; Luke 12:7
4. Gen. 25:29–34.
5. George Washington Carver (1861?–1943) was an agricultural chemist and agronomist whose work helped revolutionize the agricultural economy of the American South and won him international acclaim. He was visited by presidents Calvin Coolidge and Franklin D. Roosevelt, and counted Henry Ford and Mohandas Gandhi among his friends.

6. Henry Wadsworth Longfellow, "A Psalm of Life"; Chananda, "Solar Manifestations of the Living God," *Pearls of Wisdom,* vol. 11, no. 30, July 28, 1968.

7. H. P. Blavatsky, *The Secret Doctrine,* vol. 1, *Cosmogenesis* (1888; reprint, Passadena, Calif.: Theosophical University Press, 1977), p. 63. A *manvantara* (Sanskrit) is one of the fourteen intervals in Hinduism that constitute a *kalpa,* the period of time covering a cosmic cycle from the origination to the destruction of a world system.

8. The terms God and Goddess denote that they are Cosmic Beings who ensoul the God consciousness of their level in the Hierarchy of the Great White Brotherhood.

9. During the long winter at Valley Forge, Micah, the Angel of Unity, appeared to George Washington in a vision of three great perils that would come upon the nation of America—the Revolutionary War, the War between the States and a third world conflict. According to Anthony Sherman's account of this vision, Washington related that he was shown the inhabitants of America "in battle array against each other. As I continued looking I saw a bright angel, on whose brow rested a crown of light, on which was traced the word 'Union,' bearing the American flag which he placed between the divided nation, and said, 'Remember ye are brethren.' Instantly, the inhabitants, casting from them their weapons, became friends once more and united around the National Standard." (*Saint Germain On Alchemy* [Corwin Springs, Mont.: Summit University Press, 1993], pp. 142–51.)

10. Henry Wadsworth Longfellow, *The Song of Hiawatha,* Part 1: "The Peace Pipe."

11. *E pluribus unum* (Latin, "one out of many"): the original motto adopted for the Great Seal of the United States. It refers to the American determination to form a unified nation from people of diverse beliefs and backgrounds.

12. Rev. 1:8; 21:6; 22:13.

13. Afra, "The Powers and Perils of Nationhood," in *Afra: Brother of Light* (Corwin Springs, Mont.: The Summit Lighthouse Library, 2002).

14. Ibid.

Section III • Outlines on the Mirror...

Opening quotation: Mark 3:35.

1. Excerpted from Mark L. Prophet and Elizabeth Clare Prophet, *The Lost Teachings of Jesus,* Book One (Corwin Springs, Mont.: Summit University Press, 1994), chapter 1.
2. Matt. 6:33.
3. Matt. 12:50.
4. Goddess Meru, "Behold the Face of God," October 14, 1972.
5. For an example of someone who embodied this principle, see *The Practice of the Presence of God,* by Brother Lawrence (New York: Phoenix Press, 1985).
6. Matt. 10:36.
7. Confucius, "The Great Learning," from *The Sacred Books and Early Literature of the East* (New York: Parke, Austin, and Lipscomb, Inc., 1917), vol. XI.
8. As well as the seven rays of the white light that emerge through the prism of the Christ consciousness, there are also five "secret rays," which originate in the white-fire core of being. Initiations of the secret rays are a refinement of the senses of the soul. "The secret rays promote an action of detail," Mighty Cosmos explains, "the final sculpturing of the mind and consciousness in the perfect image of the Christ. The secret rays are like the refiner's fire. They purge, they purify." (June 30, 1973)

    Symbolically and actually, the initiations of the five secret rays take the soul into the white-fire core of being, into the very nucleus of life, into the secret chamber of the heart where the individual stands face-to-face with the inner Guru, the beloved Christ Self, and receives the soul testings that precede the alchemical union with the Christ Self—the marriage of the bride (soul who becomes the Lamb's wife). The initiations of the five secret rays are described by Saint John of the Cross as the dark night of the soul and the dark night of the spirit, in his work "The Dark Night."
9. Paul the Venetian, "The Symmetry of the Christ Mind," *Pearls of Wisdom,* vol. 15, no. 8, February 20, 1972.
10. Gen. 1:28.
11. Matt. 6:34.
12. Gen. 2:18–22.
13. Isa. 54:5.

14. Matt. 19:6; Mark 10:9.
15. Matt. 19:12.
16. Heb. 13:4.
17. Goddess of Purity, "The Integrity and the Integration of the Allness of God," July 29, 1973.
18. There is no doubt that the population of the planet is increasing dramatically. But in reality, this so-called population explosion is nothing but the expansion of the Christ consciousness according to divine plan going all the way back to the Great Central Sun. This is the laying of the foundation for the dispensation of the Aquarian age, when souls who have been in the astral plane or the mental plane or the etheric plane for hundreds of thousands of years will once again have the opportunity to enter the Guru-chela relationship, to receive the gift of the violet flame, to balance their karma and to make their ascension.

    This "population explosion" is in fact ordained by God and sponsored for karmic reasons by our teachers of the Aquarian age, Saint Germain and his twin flame, Portia. Billions of souls need to be in embodiment together as we move from the Piscean age to the age of Aquarius. For we are reaping the karma not only of the Piscean age but also of the twelve previous ages—amounting to a total of 25,800 years.

    A worldwide drive is now under way to reduce the population growth to zero and thereby stay the wholesale famines and resulting wars that are considered to be inevitable. In commenting upon these theories we must point out certain gaps in man's understanding of his ecology. It is one thing for man to control the populations of "the fish of the sea, the fowl of the air, the cattle, and of every creeping thing"—for God placed these in his care; but it is another for him to assume this control over mankind. Although God gave to man the privilege of naming the species (Gen. 2:19) and governing their reproduction, he reserved for himself and his heavenly Hierarchy the authority of giving or withholding life among his sons and daughters evolving on earth.

    It is strange—more than strange, it is diabolical—that millions of God-fearing people should be convinced overnight by population "experts" that current growth trends represent an ever mounting swell on a graph that has no governing principle behind it, no coordinator, no God who is in control of his universe. The truth is that human life is not merely one step removed from animal life: it is another evolution entirely—an evolution of souls in the state of becoming God, an evolution programmed from the very heart of the Central Sun, whose every member, like the hairs of our heads, is numbered.

For further information on doctrines of population control and the spiritual ecology of the planet, see Mark L. Prophet and Elizabeth Clare Prophet, *Climb the Highest Mountain: The Path of the Higher Self,* chapter 7.

19. Lady Master Nada, "The Golden Age of the Family," October 11, 1974.

20. Saint Germain, "The Summoning of Forces," Part 2, *Pearls of Wisdom,* vol. 21, no. 2, January 8, 1978.

21. Mother Mary, July 3, 1960.

22. Mother Mary, *Pearls of Wisdom,* vol. 3, no. 52, December 23, 1960.

23. Mother Mary, *Pearls of Wisdom,* vol. 6, no. 6, February 8, 1963.

24. Mother Mary, "The Responsibilities of Our Love," *Pearls of Wisdom,* vol. 13, no. 37, September 13, 1970.

25. Mother Mary, "Shaping the Hard Wood," *Pearls of Wisdom,* vol. 11, no. 9, March 3, 1968.

26. God Meru, "To Plead the Cause of Youth," *Pearls of Wisdom,* vol. 30, no. 19, May 10, 1987.

27. Ibid.

Section IV • "I and My Mother Are One"

Opening quotation: Exod. 20:12.

1. El Morya, February 22, 1970.

2. Mark L. Prophet and Elizabeth Clare Prophet, *My Soul Doth Magnify the Lord!* (Corwin Springs, Mont.: Summit University Press, 1986), p. 132.

3. John 17:11, 21–23.

4. Mark L. Prophet and Elizabeth Clare Prophet, *My Soul Doth Magnify the Lord!* (Corwin Springs, Mont.: Summit University Press, 1986), pp. 332–34, 340.

5. Mother Mary, September 2, 1973.

6. Mother Mary, "Many Devotees to Keep the Flame of Mother," April 14, 1974.

7. The Keepers of the Flame Fraternity is an organization of Ascended Masters and their chelas who vow to keep the flame of life on earth and support the activities of the Great White Brotherhood in the establishment of their community and mystery school and in the dissemination of their teachings. It was founded in 1961 by Saint Germain. Keepers of the Flame receive graded lessons in cosmic law dictated by the Ascended Masters to their Messengers Mark and Elizabeth Prophet.

8. Gautama Buddha, "The Torch Is Passed!" *Pearls of Wisdom,* vol. 26, no. 22, May 29, 1983.

9. 2 Cor. 12:15.

10. Sanat Kumara, "God Is Willing to Shorten the Time of Man's Travail," *Pearls of Wisdom,* vol. 42, no. 31, August 1, 1999.

11. John 8:12.

12. Mother Mary, *Pearls of Wisdom,* vol. 6, no. 1, February 15, 1963.

13. Omri-Tas, "Saturate the Earth with Violet Flame!" *Pearls of Wisdom,* vol. 27, no. 50A, October 17, 1984.

14. Casimir Poseidon, "Learn to Love to Do Well and You Shall," October 5, 1975.

15. Maria Montessori, *The Montessori Method* (New York: Frederick A. Stokes Company, 1912), p. 353.

16. Lord Lanto, October 30, 1966.

17. God Meru, July 6, 1969.

Section V • World Communism

Opening quotation: Acts 4:32.

1. John 1:5, 14.

2. Acts 2:44–45.

3. Rev. 3:16.

4. Mark L. Prophet and Elizabeth Clare Prophet, *Saint Germain on Alchemy* (Corwin Springs, Mont.: Summit University Press, 1993), pp. 310–12.

5. Karl Marx and Frederick Engels, *Manifesto of the Communist Party,* trans. Samuel Moore, part 1.

6. Phil. 2:12.

7. El Morya, *Pearls of Wisdom,* vol. 6, no. 7, February 15, 1963.

8. Chananda and Alexander Gaylord, *Keepers of the Flame Les-*

son 5, pp. 15–20.

9. The Great Divine Director, "Stellar Modes," *Keepers of the Flame Lesson 6.*
10. Luke 6:31.
11. Matt. 5:44.
12. Gal. 5:9; 1 Cor. 5:6.
13. Meta, "The Reseeding of This Age with Seeds of Righteousness," *Pearls of Wisdom,* vol. 11, no. 28, July 14, 1968.
14. Matt. 7:14.
15. Jer. 31:34; Rev. 7:17; 21:4.
16. John 14:2.
17. Lanto, "A Message from the Grand Teton Retreat," *Keepers of the Flame Lesson 9.*
18. El Morya, *Pearls of Wisdom,* vol. 6, no. 7, February 15, 1963.
19. 2 Tim. 2:15.
20. Luke 16:1–13.
21. James 1:27.
22. Lord Maitreya, "The Principle of the Abundant Life," *Pearls of Wisdom,* vol. 12, no. 43, October 26, 1969.
23. El Morya, "An Encyclical on World Goodwill," in Mark L. Prophet and Elizabeth Clare Prophet, *Morya I* (Corwin Springs, Mont.: The Summit Lighthouse Library, 2001), p. 212.
24. Omri-Tas, "Saturate the Earth with Violet Flame!" *Pearls of Wisdom,* vol. 27, no. 50A, October 17, 1984.

Section VI • The Twelve Tribes of Israel

Opening quotation: Matt. 10:6.

1. Dan. 7:9, 13, 22.
2. James 2:23.
3. Gen. 12:2.
4. Gen. 15:5.
5. Gen. 15:12–16.
6. Gen. 26:2–5.
7. Gen. 28:12–14.
8. Gen. 32:24–28.
9. Gen. 37:3.
10. Gen. 48:5.
11. Gen. 48:21.
12. Deut. 31:19–21.

13. Heb. 8:12.
14. 1 Sam. 8:5.
15. Jer. 4:6.
16. Jer. 32:35.
17. Matt. 10:6.
18. Exod. 3:15.
19. Numbers 21:8.
20. Kuthumi and Djwal Kul, *The Human Aura* (Corwin Springs, Mont.: Summit University Press, 1996), Book Two, Chapter 11.
21. See, for example, Raymond Capt, *Jacob's Pillar* (Thousand Oaks, Calif.: Artisan Sales, 1977); Colonel J. C. Gawler, *Dan: Pioneer of Israel* (Thousand Oaks, Calif.: Artisan Sales, 1984).
22. Exod. 3:14.
23. Matt. 24:31; Mark 13:27.
24. Thirty-three centuries ago, Ikhnaton, pharaoh of Egypt (c. 1375–1358 B.C.), introduced a revolutionary monotheism based on the worship of one God, 'Aton'—represented in the symbol of a sun disk or orb with diverging rays, each ending in a hand. Ikhnaton believed that everything that lived had its being through the sun's rays and that he himself was the son of Aton.
25. Saint Patrick, April 3, 1977.

Section VII • The Twelve Apostles

Opening quotation: Matt. 4:19.

1. John 20:17.
2. Luke 24:49.
3. Matt. 7:29; Mark 1:22.
4. John's Gospel describes what is apparently the first meeting of Jesus with any of the disciples, and Andrew is the first disciple named in this account (John 1:38). Early Byzantine tradition therefore names Andrew *Protokletos*, "first called."
5. John 1:36.
6. Matt. 4:15–22; Mark 1:16–20.
7. Matt. 3:17; Mark 1:11.
8. John 1:43–45.
9. John 11:16.
10. John 20:24–29.
11. Jesus, "The Igniting of Joy," *Pearls of Wisdom*, vol. 35, no. 67, December 20, 1992.

12. John 1:42.
13. Matt. 16:13–18.
14. Heb. 13:8.
15. Mother Mary, "Divine Wholeness: My Definition of Church," *Pearls of Wisdom*, vol. 24, no. 71, August 1981.
16. Luke 22:31.
17. Matt. 26:75; Mark 14:72; Luke 22:61–62; John 18:27.
18. Luke 5:8.
19. John 1:45–51.
20. Matt. 9:9; Mark 2:14; Luke 5:27–28.
21. Matt. 9:10–12; Mark 2:15–17; Luke 5:30–32.
22. John 14:22–23.
23. Gal. 2:9; Acts 15:1–29.
24. John 13:25–27.
25. John 19:27.
26. Dan. 3:20–26.
27. Rev. Alban Butler, *The Lives of the Fathers, Martyrs and Other Principal Saints*, vol. IV, s.v. "St. John the Evangelist."
28. *Butler's Lives of the Saints*, edited, revised and supplemented by Herbert Thurston and Donald Attwater (New York: D. J. Kennedy & Sons, 1956), vol. IV, p. 622.
29. Acts 1:23–26.

Section VIII • Christ, the Immaculate Concept

Opening quotation: Matt. 16:18.
1. 1 Cor. 12:10.
2. Lanello, "The Covenant of Compassion," *Pearls of Wisdom*, vol. 27, no. 35, July 1, 1984.
3. Saint Germain, "The Individual Path," *Pearls of Wisdom*, vol. 31, no. 50, August 13, 1988.
4. James 1:27.
5. 1984 *Pearls of Wisdom*, Book 2, Introduction II, pp. 9–12.
6. Ps. 139:7, 8.
7. 1984 *Pearls of Wisdom*, Book 2, Introduction II, pp. 12–13.
8. 1984 *Pearls of Wisdom*, Book 2, Introduction II, pp. 13–14.
9. In a dictation given on October 31, 1975, Serapis said: "Come forth in an orderly manner so that the Mother may touch your third eye with the amethyst egg that I have already charged with the ascension flame for the sealing of the third eye from

all misuses of the sacred fire." Following this dictation, the congregation was invited to pass before the Messenger to receive the touch of the amethyst egg upon the heart.

10. John 1:9.
11. Lord Maitreya, "Expect the Unexpected," *Pearls of Wisdom,* vol. 43, no. 26, June 25, 2000.
12. 1984 *Pearls of Wisdom,* Book 2, Introduction II, p. 66.
13. Eccles. 1:2; 12:8.
14. Isa. 1:18.
15. John 10:10.
16. Jesus, "The Caravan of the Ages," December 31, 1972.
17. Matt. 25:40; Matt. 18:10.
18. Matt. 7:1–2.
19. El Morya, "A Report," *Pearls of Wisdom,* vol. 5, no. 43, October 26, 1962.
20. Mark 10:42–44.
21. Serapis Bey, "A Message from the Hierarch of Luxor on Certain Disciplines of the Keepers of the Flame," Keepers of the Flame Lesson 2, pp. 1–2.
22. Matt. 16:18.
23. Rev. 2:17.
24. Hilarion, "On the Church Today," *Pearls of Wisdom,* vol. 34, no. 21, May 26, 1991.
25. Rev. 2:17.
26. Eph. 2:20.
27. Matt. 24:15; Mark 13:14.
28. Dan. 7:9.
29. Pope John XXIII, "The Church Universal and Triumphant," *Keepers of the Flame Lesson 10,* p. 24.
30. See El Morya, "The Pillars of Eternity," *Pearls of Wisdom,* vol. 14, no. 19, May 9, 1971.
31. El Morya, "The Universal Religion," *Pearls of Wisdom,* vol. 28, no. 51, December 22, 1985.
32. Matt. 25:37–40; El Morya, *Pearls of Wisdom,* vol. 6, no. 7, February 15, 1963.

Glossary

Terms set in italics are defined elsewhere in the glossary.

Adept. An initiate of the *Great White Brotherhood* of a high degree of attainment, especially in the control of *Matter,* physical forces, nature spirits and bodily functions; fully the alchemist undergoing advanced initiations of the *sacred fire* on the path of the *ascension.*

Akashic records. The impressions of all that has ever transpired in the physical universe, recorded in the etheric substance and dimension known by the Sanskrit term *akasha.* These records can be read by those with developed *soul* faculties.

Alchemical marriage. The soul's permanent bonding to the *Holy Christ Self,* in preparation for the permanent fusing to the *I AM Presence* in the ritual of the ascension. See also *Soul; Secret chamber of the heart.*

All-Seeing Eye of God. See *Cyclopea.*

Alpha and Omega. The divine wholeness of the Father-Mother God affirmed as "the beginning and the ending" by the Lord Christ in Revelation (Rev. 1:8, 11; 21:6; 22:13). Ascended *twin flames* of the *Cosmic Christ* consciousness who hold the balance of the masculine-feminine polarity of the Godhead in the *Great Central Sun* of cosmos. Thus through the *Universal Christ* (the *Word* incarnate), the Father is the origin and the Mother is the fulfillment of the cycles of God's consciousness expressed throughout the *Spirit-Matter* creation. See also *Mother.*

Ancient of Days. See *Sanat Kumara.*

Angel. A divine spirit, a herald or messenger sent by God to deliver his *Word* to his children. A ministering spirit sent forth to tend the heirs of *Christ*—to comfort, protect, guide, strengthen, teach, counsel and warn. The fallen angels, also called the dark ones, are those angels who followed Lucifer in the Great Rebellion, whose consciousness therefore "fell" to lower levels of vibration. They were "cast out into the earth" by Archangel Michael (Rev. 12:7-12)—constrained by the karma of their disobedience to God and his Christ to take on and evolve through dense physical bodies. Here they walk about, sowing seeds of unrest and rebellion among men and nations.

Antahkarana. The web of life. The net of *light* spanning *Spirit* and *Matter,* connecting and sensitizing the whole of creation within itself and to the heart of God.

Archangel. The highest rank in the orders of *angels.* Each of the *seven rays* has a presiding Archangel who, with his divine complement, or Archeia, embodies the God consciousness of the ray and directs the bands of angels serving in their command on that ray. The Archangels and Archeiai of the rays and the locations of their *retreats* are as follows:

First ray, blue, Archangel Michael and Faith, Banff, near Lake Louise, Alberta, Canada.

Second ray, yellow, Archangel Jophiel and Christine, south of the Great Wall near Lanchow, north central China.

Third ray, petal pink, deep rose and ruby, Archangel Chamuel and Charity, St. Louis, Missouri, U.S.A.

Fourth ray, white and mother-of-pearl, Archangel Gabriel and Hope, between Sacramento and Mount Shasta, California, U.S.A.

Fifth ray, green, Archangel Raphael and Mary, Fátima, Portugal.

Sixth ray, purple and gold with ruby flecks, Archangel Uriel and

Aurora, Tatra Mountains, south of Cracow, Poland.

Seventh ray, violet and purple, Archangel Zadkiel and Holy Amethyst, Cuba.

Archeia (pl. **Archeiai**). Divine complement and *twin flame* of an *Archangel.*

Ascended Master. One who, through *Christ* and the putting on of that Mind which was in Christ Jesus (Phil. 2:5), has mastered time and space and in the process gained the mastery of the self in the *four lower bodies* and the four quadrants of *Matter,* in the *chakras* and the balanced *threefold flame.* An Ascended Master has also transmuted at least 51 percent of his karma, fulfilled his divine plan, and taken the initiations of the ruby ray unto the ritual of the *ascension*—acceleration by the *sacred fire* into the Presence of the I AM THAT I AM (the *I AM Presence*). Ascended Masters inhabit the planes of *Spirit*—the kingdom of God (God's consciousness)—and they may teach unascended souls in an *etheric temple* or in the cities on the *etheric plane* (the kingdom of heaven).

Ascension. The ritual whereby the *soul* reunites with the *Spirit* of the living God, the *I AM Presence.* The ascension is the culmination of the soul's God-victorious sojourn in time and space. It is the process whereby the soul, having balanced her karma and fulfilled her divine plan, merges first with the Christ consciousness and then with the living Presence of the I AM THAT I AM. Once the ascension has taken place, the soul—the corruptible aspect of being—becomes the incorruptible one, a permanent atom in the body of God. See also *Alchemical marriage.*

Aspirant. One who aspires; specifically, one who aspires to reunion with God through the ritual of the *ascension.* One who aspires to overcome the conditions and limitations of time and space to fulfill the cycles of karma and one's reason for being through the sacred labor.

Astral plane. A frequency of time and space beyond the physical, yet below the mental, corresponding to the *emotional body* of man and the collective unconscious of the race; the repository of mankind's thoughts and feelings, conscious and unconscious. Because the astral plane has been muddied by impure human thought and feeling, the term "astral" is often used in a negative context to refer to that which is impure or psychic.

Astrea. Feminine Elohim of the fourth ray, the ray of purity, who works to cut *souls* free from the *astral plane* and the projections of the dark forces. See also *Elohim; Seven rays.*

Atman. The spark of the Divine within, identical with *Brahman;* the ultimate essence of the universe as well as the essence of the individual.

AUM. See *OM.*

Avatar. The incarnation of the *Word.* The avatar of an age is the *Christ,* the incarnation of the Son of God. The *Manus* may designate numerous Christed ones—those endued with an extraordinary *light*—to go forth as world teachers and wayshowers. The Christed ones demonstrate in a given epoch the law of the *Logos,* stepped down through the Manu(s) and the avatar(s) until it is made flesh through their own word and work—to be ultimately victorious in its fulfillment in all souls of light sent forth to conquer time and space in that era.

Bodhisattva. (Sanskrit, 'a being of *bodhi,* or enlightenment.') A being destined for enlightenment, or one whose energy and power is directed toward enlightenment. A Bodhisattva is destined to become a *Buddha* but has forgone the bliss of *nirvana* with a vow to save all children of God on earth. An Ascended Master or an unascended master may be a Bodhisattva.

Brahman. Ultimate Reality; the Absolute.

Buddha. (From Sanskrit *budh* 'awake, know, perceive.') "The enlightened one." Buddha denotes an office in the spiritual *Hierarchy* of worlds that is attained by passing certain initiations of the *sacred fire,* including those of the *seven rays* of the Holy Spirit and of the five secret *rays,* the raising of the feminine ray (sacred fire of the *Kundalini*) and the "mastery of the seven in the seven multiplied by the power of the ten."

Gautama attained the enlightenment of the Buddha twenty-five centuries ago, a path he had pursued through many previous embodiments culminating in his forty-nine-day meditation under the Bo tree. Hence he is called Gautama, the Buddha. He holds the office of *Lord of the World,* sustaining, by his *Causal Body* and *threefold flame,* the divine spark and consciousness in the evolutions of earth approaching the path of personal Christhood. His aura of love/wisdom ensouling the planet issues from his incomparable devotion to the Divine *Mother.* He is the Hierarch of Shamballa, the original *retreat* of *Sanat Kumara* now on the *etheric plane* over the Gobi Desert.

Lord Maitreya, the *Cosmic Christ,* has also passed the initiations of the Buddha. He is the long-awaited Coming Buddha who has come to the fore to teach all who have departed from the way of the Great *Guru,* Sanat Kumara, from whose lineage both he and Gautama descended. In the history of the planet, there have been numerous Buddhas who have served the evolutions of mankind through the steps and stages of the path of the *Bodhisattva.* In the East Jesus is referred to as the Buddha Issa. He is the World Saviour by the love/wisdom of the Godhead.

Caduceus. The Kundalini. See *Sacred fire.*

Causal Body. Seven concentric spheres of *light* surrounding the *I AM Presence.* The spheres of the Causal Body contain the records of the virtuous acts we have performed to the glory of God and the blessing of man through our many incarnations on earth. See also *Chart of Your Divine Self.*

Central Sun. A vortex of energy, physical or spiritual, central to systems of worlds that it thrusts from, or gathers unto, itself by the Central Sun Magnet. Whether in the *microcosm* or the *Macrocosm,* the Central Sun is the principal energy source, vortex, or nexus of energy interchange in atoms, cells, man (the heart center), amidst plant life and the core of the earth. The Great Central Sun is the center of cosmos; the point of integration of the *Spirit-Matter* cosmos; the point of origin of all physical-spiritual creation; the nucleus, or white-fire core, of the *Cosmic Egg.* (The God Star, Sirius, is the focus of the Great Central Sun in our sector of the galaxy.) The Sun behind the sun is the spiritual Cause behind the physical effect we see as our own physical sun and all other stars and star systems, seen or unseen, including the Great Central Sun.

Chakra. (Sanskrit, 'wheel, disc, circle.') Center of light anchored in the etheric body and governing the flow of energy to the four lower bodies of man. There are seven major chakras corresponding to the seven rays, five minor chakras corresponding to the five secret rays, and a total of 144 light centers in the body of man.

Chart of Your Divine Self. There are three figures represented in the Chart. The upper figure is the *I AM Presence,* the I AM THAT I AM, the individualization of God's Presence for every son and daughter of the Most High. The Divine Monad consists of the I AM Presence surrounded by the spheres (color rings) of *light* that make up the body of First Cause, or *Causal Body.*

The middle figure in the Chart is the Mediator between God and man, called the *Holy Christ Self,* the *Real Self* or the *Christ* consciousness. It has also been referred to as the Higher Mental Body or one's Higher Consciousness. This Inner Teacher overshadows the lower self, which consists of the soul evolving through the four planes of *Matter* using the vehicles of the *four lower bodies*—the *etheric* (memory) body, the *mental body,* the *emotional* (desire) *body,* and the *physical body*—to balance karma and fulfill the divine plan.

The three figures of the Chart correspond to the Trinity of Father (who always includes the *Mother*), Son (the middle figure) and Holy Spirit (the lower figure). The latter is the intended temple of the Holy Spirit, whose *sacred fire* is indicated in the enfolding *violet flame.* The lower figure corresponds to you as a disciple on the *Path.*

The lower figure is surrounded by a *tube of light,* which is projected from the heart of the I AM Presence in answer to your call. It is a cylinder of white light that sustains a forcefield of protection twenty-four hours a day, so long as you guard it in harmony. The *threefold flame* of life is the divine spark sent from the I AM Presence as the gift of life, consciousness and free will. It is sealed in the *secret chamber of the heart* that through the love, wisdom and power of the Godhead anchored therein the *soul* may fulfill her reason for being in the physical plane. Also called the Christ Flame and the Liberty Flame, or fleur-de-lis, it is the spark of a man's divinity, his potential for Christhood.

The silver cord (or *crystal cord*) is the stream of life, or *lifestream,* that descends from the heart of the I AM Presence to the Holy Christ Self to nourish and sustain (through the *chakras*) the soul and its vehicles of expression in time and space. It is over this 'umbilical cord' that the energy of the Presence flows, entering the being of man at the crown and giving impetus for the pulsation of the threefold flame as well as the physical heartbeat.

When a round of the soul's incarnation in Matter-form is finished, the I AM Presence withdraws the silver cord (Eccles. 12:6), whereupon the threefold flame returns to the level of the Christ, and the soul clothed in the etheric garment gravitates to the highest level of her attainment, where she is schooled between embodiments until her final incarnation when the Great Law decrees she shall go out no more.

The dove of the Holy Spirit descending from the heart of the Father is shown just above the head of the Christ. When the son of man puts on and becomes the Christ consciousness as Jesus did, he merges with the Holy Christ Self. The Holy Spirit is upon him, and the words of the Father, the beloved I AM Presence, are spoken: "This is my beloved Son, in whom I AM well pleased" (Matt. 3:17).

Chela. (Hindi *celā* from Sanskrit *ceṭa* 'slave,' i.e., 'servant.') In India, a disciple of a religious teacher or *guru.* A term used generally to refer to a student of the *Ascended Masters* and their teachings. Specifically, a student of more than ordinary self-discipline and devotion initiated by an Ascended Master and serving the cause of the *Great White Brotherhood.*

Chohan. (Tibetan, 'lord' or 'master'; a chief.) Each of the seven *rays* has a Chohan who focuses the *Christ* consciousness of the ray. Having ensouled and demonstrated the law of the ray throughout numerous incarnations, and having taken initiations both before and after the *ascension,* the candidate is appointed to the office of Chohan by the Maha Chohan (the "Great Lord"), who is himself the representative of the Holy Spirit on all the rays. The names of the Chohans of the Rays (each one an *Ascended Master* representing one of the seven rays to earth's evolutions) and the locations of their physical/etheric focuses are as follows:

First ray, El Morya, Retreat of God's Will, Darjeeling, India.

Second ray, Lanto, Royal Teton Retreat, Grand Teton, Jackson Hole, Wyoming, U.S.A.

Third ray, Paul the Venetian, Château de Liberté, southern France, with a focus of the *threefold flame* at the Washington Monument, Washington, D.C., U.S.A.

Fourth ray, Serapis Bey, the Ascension Temple and Retreat at Luxor, Egypt.

Fifth ray, Hilarion (the apostle Paul), Temple of Truth, Crete.

Sixth ray, Nada, Arabian Retreat, Saudi Arabia.

Seventh ray, Saint Germain, Royal Teton Retreat, Grand Teton, Wyoming, U.S.A.; Cave of Symbols, Table Mountain, Wyoming, U.S.A. Saint Germain also works out of the Great Divine Director's focuses—the Cave of Light in India and the Rakoczy Mansion in Transylvania, where Saint Germain presides as Hierarch.

Christ. (From the Greek *Christos* 'anointed.') Messiah (Hebrew, Aramaic 'anointed'); 'Christed one,' one fully endued and infilled—anointed—by the *light* (the Son) of God. The *Word,* the *Logos,* the Second Person of the Trinity. In the Hindu Trinity of Brahma, Vishnu and Shiva, the term "Christ" corresponds to or is the incarnation of Vishnu, the Preserver; Avatâra, God-man, Dispeller of Darkness, *Guru.*

The term "Christ" or "Christed one" also denotes an office in *Hierarchy* held by those who have attained self-mastery on the *seven rays* and the seven *chakras* of the Holy Spirit. Christ-mastery includes the balancing of the *threefold flame*—the divine attributes of power, wisdom and love—for the harmonization of consciousness and the implementation of the mastery of the seven rays in the chakras and in the *four lower bodies* through the Mother Flame (the raised *Kundalini*).

At the hour designated for the *ascension,* the *soul* thus anointed raises the spiral of the threefold flame from beneath the feet through the entire form for the transmutation of every atom and cell of her being, consciousness and world. The saturation and acceleration of the *four lower bodies* and the soul by this transfiguring light of the Christ Flame take place in part during the initiation of the *transfiguration,* increasing through the resurrection and gaining full intensity in the ritual of the ascension.

Christ Self. The individualized focus of "the only begotten of the Father, full of grace and Truth." The *Universal Christ* individualized as the true identity of the *soul;* the *Real Self* of every man, woman and child, to which the soul must rise. The Christ Self is the Mediator between a man and his God. He is a man's own personal teacher, master and prophet.

Color rays. See *Seven rays.*

Cosmic Being. (1) An *Ascended Master* who has attained cosmic consciousness and ensouls the *light*/energy/consciousness of many worlds and systems of worlds across the galaxies to the Sun behind the *Great Central Sun;* or, (2) A being of God who has never descended below the level of the *Christ,* has never taken physical embodiment, and has never made human karma.

Cosmic Christ. An office in *Hierarchy* currently held by Lord Maitreya under Gautama *Buddha,* the *Lord of the World.* Also used as a synonym for *Universal Christ.*

Cosmic Clock. The science of charting the cycles of the *soul's* karma and initiations on the twelve lines of the Clock under the *Twelve Hierarchies of the Sun.* Taught by Mother Mary to Mark and Elizabeth Prophet for sons and daughters of God returning to the Law of the One and to their point of origin beyond the worlds of form and lesser causation.

Cosmic Egg. The spiritual-material universe, including a seemingly endless chain of galaxies, star systems, worlds known and unknown, whose center, or white-fire core, is called the *Great Central Sun*. The Cosmic Egg has both a spiritual and a material center. Although we may discover and observe the Cosmic Egg from the standpoint of our physical senses and perspective, all of the dimensions of *Spirit* can also be known and experienced within the Cosmic Egg. For the God who created the Cosmic Egg and holds it in the hollow of his hand is also the God Flame expanding hour by hour within his very own sons and daughters. The Cosmic Egg represents the bounds of man's habitation in this cosmic cycle. Yet, as God is everywhere throughout and beyond the Cosmic Egg, so by his Spirit within us we daily awaken to new dimensions of being, soul-satisfied in conformity with his likeness.

Cosmic Law. The Law that governs mathematically, yet with the spontaneity of Mercy's flame, all manifestation throughout the cosmos in the planes of Spirit and Matter.

Crystal cord. The stream of God's light, life and consciousness that nourishes and sustains the soul and her four lower bodies. Also called the silver cord (Eccles. 12:6). See also *Chart of Your Divine Self*.

Cyclopea. Masculine Elohim of the fifth ray, also known as the All-Seeing Eye of God or as the Great Silent Watcher. See also *Elohim; Seven rays*.

Deathless solar body. See *Seamless garment*.

Decree. A dynamic form of spoken prayer used by students of the *Ascended Masters* to direct God's *light* into individual and world conditions. The decree may be short or long and is usually marked by a formal preamble and a closing or acceptance. It is the authoritative *Word* of God spoken in man in the name of the *I AM Presence* and the living *Christ* to bring about constructive change on earth through the will of God. The decree is the birthright of the sons and daughters of God, the "Command ye me" of Isaiah 45:11, the original fiat of the Creator: "Let there be light: and there was light" (Gen. 1:3). It is written in the Book of Job, "Thou shalt decree a thing, and it shall be established unto thee: and the light shall shine upon thy ways" (Job 22:28).

Dictation. A message from an *Ascended Master,* an *Archangel* or another advanced spiritual being delivered through the agency of the Holy Spirit by a *Messenger* of the *Great White Brotherhood.*

Divine Monad. See *Chart of Your Divine Self; I AM Presence.*

Electronic Presence. A duplicate of the *I AM Presence* of an Ascended Master.

Elohim. (Hebrew; plural of *Eloah,* 'God.') The name of God used in the first verse of the Bible: "In the beginning God created the heaven and the earth." The Seven Mighty Elohim and their feminine counterparts are the builders of form. They are the "seven spirits of God" named in Revelation 4:5 and the "morning stars" that sang together in the beginning, as the Lord revealed them to Job (Job 38:7). In the order of *Hierarchy,* the Elohim and *Cosmic Beings* carry the greatest concentration, the highest vibration of *light* that we can comprehend in our present state of evolution. Serving directly under the Elohim are the four hierarchs of the elements, who have dominion over the elementals—the gnomes, salamanders, sylphs and undines.

Following are the names of the Seven Elohim and their divine complements, the ray they serve on and the location of their etheric *retreat:*

First ray, Hercules and Amazonia, Half Dome, Sierra Nevada, Yosemite National Park, California, U.S.A.

Second ray, Apollo and Lumina, western Lower Saxony, Germany.

Third ray, Heros and Amora, Lake Winnipeg, Manitoba, Canada.

Fourth ray, Purity and *Astrea,* near Gulf of Archangel, southeast arm of White Sea, Russia.

Fifth ray, *Cyclopea* and Virginia, Altai Range where China, Siberia and Mongolia meet, near Tabun Bogdo.

Sixth ray, Peace and Aloha, Hawaiian Islands.

Seventh ray, Arcturus and Victoria, near Luanda, Angola, Africa.

Emotional body. One of the *four lower bodies* of man, corresponding to the water element and the third quadrant of *Matter;* the vehicle of the desires and feelings of God made manifest in the being of man. Also called the astral body, the desire body or the feeling body.

Entity. A conglomerate of misqualified energy or disembodied individuals who have chosen to embody evil. Entities that are focuses of sinister forces may attack disembodied as well as embodied individuals.

Etheric body. One of the *four lower bodies* of man, corresponding to the fire element and the first quadrant of *Matter;* called the envelope of the *soul,* holding the blueprint of the divine plan and the image of *Christ*-perfection to be outpictured in the world of form. Also called the memory body.

Etheric octave or etheric plane. The highest plane in the dimension of *Matter;* a plane that is as concrete and real as the physical plane (and even more so) but is experienced through the senses of the *soul* in a dimension and a consciousness beyond physical awareness. This is the plane on which the *akashic records* of mankind's entire evolution register individually and collectively. It is the world of *Ascended Masters* and their *retreats,* etheric cities of *light* where *souls* of a higher order of evolution abide between embodiments. It is the plane of Reality.

The lower *etheric plane,* which overlaps the astral/mental/physical belts, is contaminated by these lower worlds occupied by the false hierarchy and the mass consciousness it controls.

Etheric temple. See *Retreat.*

Fallen angels. See *Angels.*

Father-Mother God. See *Alpha and Omega.*

Four Cosmic Forces. The four beasts seen by Saint John and other seers as the lion, the calf (or ox), the man and the flying eagle (Rev. 4:6–8; Ezek. 1:10). They sustain the vision of the LORD God Almighty as universal awareness of the Creator within the creation. They render the light, the energy of the Word, intelligible to electrons small and great in man and beast, vegetable and mineral.

Four lower bodies. Four sheaths of four distinct frequencies that surround the soul (the physical, emotional, mental and etheric bodies), providing vehicles for the soul in her journey through time and space. The etheric sheath, highest in vibration, is the gateway to the three higher bodies: the *Christ Self,* the *I AM Presence* and the *Causal Body.* See also *Physical body; Emotional body; Mental body; Etheric body.*

Great Central Sun. See *Central Sun.*

Great Hub. See *Central Sun.*

Great White Brotherhood. A spiritual order of Western saints and Eastern adepts who have reunited with the *Spirit* of the living God; the heavenly hosts. They have transcended the cycles of karma and rebirth and ascended (accelerated) into that higher reality which is the eternal abode of the soul. The *Ascended Masters* of the Great White Brotherhood, united for the highest purposes of the brotherhood of man under the Fatherhood of God, have risen in every age from every culture and religion to inspire creative achievement in education, the arts and sciences, God-government and the abundant life through the economies of the nations. The word "white" refers not to race but to the aura (halo) of white *light* surrounding their forms. The Brotherhood also includes in its ranks certain unascended *chelas* of the Ascended Masters.

Guru. (Sanskrit.) A personal religious teacher and spiritual guide; one of high attainment. A guru may be unascended or ascended.

Hierarchy. The universal chain of individualized God-free beings fulfilling the attributes and aspects of God's infinite Selfhood. Included in the cosmic hierarchical scheme are *Solar Logoi, Elohim,* Sons and Daughters of God, ascended and unascended masters with their circles of *chelas, Cosmic Beings,* the *Twelve Hierarchies of the Sun, Archangels* and *angels* of the *sacred fire,* children of the *light,* nature spirits (called elementals) and *twin flames* of the *Alpha-Omega* polarity sponsoring planetary and galactic systems.

This universal order of the Father's own Self-expression is the means whereby God in the *Great Central Sun* steps down the Presence and power of his universal being/consciousness in order that succeeding evolutions in time and space, from the least unto the greatest, might come to know the wonder of his love. The level of one's spiritual/physical attainment—measured by one's balanced self-awareness "hid with *Christ* in God" and demonstrating his Law, by his love, in the *Spirit-Matter* cosmos—is the criterion establishing one's placement on this ladder of life called Hierarchy.

Higher Mental Body. See *Chart of Your Divine Self.*

Higher Self. The *I AM Presence;* the *Christ Self;* the exalted aspect of Selfhood. Used in contrast to the term "lower self," or "little self," which indicates the *soul* that went forth from and may elect by free will to return to the Divine Whole through the realization of the oneness of the Self in God. Higher consciousness.

Holy Christ Self. See *Christ Self.*

Human monad. The entire forcefield of self; the interconnecting spheres of influences—hereditary, environmental, karmic—which make up that self-awareness that identifies itself as human. The reference point of lesser- or non-awareness out of which all mankind must evolve to the realization of the *Real Self* as the *Christ Self.*

I AM Presence. The I AM THAT I AM (Exod. 3:13–15); the individualized Presence of God focused for each individual *soul.* The God-identity of the individual; the Divine Monad; the individual Source. The origin of the soul focused in the planes of *Spirit* just above the physical form; the personification of the God Flame for the individual. See also *Chart of Your Divine Self.*

I AM THAT I AM. See *I AM Presence.*

Kali Yuga. (Sanskrit.) Term in Hindu mystic philosophy for the last and worst of the four yugas (world ages), characterized by strife, discord and moral deterioration.

Karmic Board. See *Lords of Karma.*

Keepers of the Flame Fraternity. Founded in 1961 by Saint Germain, an organization of *Ascended Masters* and their *chelas* who vow to keep the flame of life on earth and to support the activities of the *Great White Brotherhood* in the establishment of their community and mystery school and in the dissemination of their teachings. Keepers of the Flame receive graded lessons in *cosmic law* dictated by the *Ascended Masters* to their *Messengers* Mark and Elizabeth Prophet.

Kundalini. See *Sacred fire.*

Lifestream. The stream of life that comes forth from the one Source, from the *I AM Presence* in the planes of *Spirit,* and descends to the planes of *Matter* where it manifests as the *threefold flame* anchored in the heart *chakra* for the sustainment of the *soul* in Matter and the nourishment of the *four lower bodies.* Used to denote souls evolving as individual "lifestreams" and hence synonymous with the term "individual." Denotes the ongoing nature of the individual through cycles of individualization.

Light. The energy of God; the potential of the *Christ.* As the personification of *Spirit,* the term "light" can be used synonymously with the terms "God" and "Christ." As the essence of Spirit, it is synonymous with *"sacred fire."* It is the emanation of the *Great Central Sun* and the individualized *I AM Presence*—and the Source of all life.

Logos. (Greek, 'word, speech, reason.') The divine wisdom manifest in the creation. According to ancient Greek philosophy, the Logos is the controlling principle in the universe. The Book of John identifies the *Word,* or Logos, with Jesus Christ: "And the Word was made flesh, and dwelt among us" (John 1:14). Hence, Jesus Christ is seen as the embodiment of divine reason, the Word Incarnate.

Lord of the World. *Sanat Kumara* held the office of Lord of the World (referred to as "God of the earth" in Rev. 11:4) for tens of thousands of years. Gautama Buddha recently succeeded Sanat Kumara and now holds this office. His is the highest governing office of the spiritual *Hierarchy* for the planet—and yet Lord Gautama is truly the most humble among the *Ascended Masters.* At inner levels, he sustains the *threefold flame,* the divine spark, for those *lifestreams* who have lost the direct contact with their *I AM Presence* and who have made so much negative karma as to be unable to magnetize sufficient *light* from the Godhead to sustain their *soul's* physical incarnation on earth. Through a filigree thread of light connecting his heart with the hearts of all God's children, Lord Gautama nourishes the flickering flame of life that ought to burn upon the altar of each heart with a greater magnitude of love, wisdom and power, fed by each one's own Christ consciousness.

Lords of Karma. The Ascended Beings who comprise the Karmic Board. Their names and the *rays* that they represent on the board are as follows: first ray, the Great Divine Director; second ray, the Goddess of Liberty; third ray, the Ascended Lady Master Nada; fourth ray, the *Elohim Cyclopea;* fifth ray, Pallas Athena, Goddess of Truth; sixth ray, Portia, Goddess of Justice; seventh ray, Kuan Yin, Goddess of Mercy. The Buddha Vairochana also sits on the Karmic Board.

The Lords of Karma dispense justice to this system of worlds, adjudicating karma, mercy and judgment on behalf of every *lifestream.* All *souls* must pass before the Karmic Board before and after each incarnation on earth, receiving their assignment and karmic allotment for each lifetime beforehand and the review of their performance at its conclusion. Through the Keeper of the Scrolls and the recording angels, the Lords of Karma have access to the complete records of every lifestream's incarnations on earth. They determine who shall embody, as well as when and where. They assign souls to families and communities, measuring out the weights of karma that must be balanced as the "jot and tittle" of the Law. The Karmic Board, acting in consonance with the individual *I AM Presence* and *Christ Self,* determines when the soul has earned the right to be free from the wheel of karma and the round of rebirth.

The Lords of Karma meet at the Royal Teton Retreat twice yearly, at winter and summer solstice, to review petitions from unascended mankind and to grant dispensations for their assistance.

Macrocosm. (Greek, 'great world.') The larger cosmos; the entire warp and woof of creation, which we call the *Cosmic Egg*. Also used to contrast man as the microcosm ('little world') against the backdrop of the larger world in which he lives. See also *Microcosm*.

Mantra. A mystical formula or invocation; a word or formula, often in Sanskrit, to be recited or sung for the purpose of intensifying the action of the *Spirit* of God in man. A form of prayer consisting of a word or a group of words that is chanted over and over again to magnetize a particular aspect of the Deity or of a being who has actualized that aspect of the Deity. See also *Decree*.

Manu. (Sanskrit.) The progenitor and lawgiver of the evolutions of God on earth. The Manu and his divine complement are *twin flames* assigned by the *Father-Mother* God to sponsor and ensoul the Christic image for a certain evolution or lifewave known as a root race—*souls* who embody as a group and have a unique archetypal pattern, divine plan and mission to fulfill on earth.

According to esoteric tradition, there are seven primary aggregations of souls—that is, the first to the seventh root races. The first three root races lived in purity and innocence upon earth in three Golden Ages before the Fall of Adam and Eve. Through obedience to *cosmic law* and total identification with the *Real Self*, these three root races won their immortal freedom and ascended from earth.

It was during the time of the fourth root race, on the continent of Lemuria, that the allegorical Fall took place under the influence of the fallen *angels* known as Serpents (because they used the serpentine spinal energies to beguile the soul, or female principle in mankind, as a means to their end of lowering the masculine potential, thereby emasculating the Sons of God).

The fourth, fifth and sixth root races (the latter soul group not having entirely descended into physical incarnation) remain in embodiment on earth today. Lord Himalaya and his beloved are the Manus for the fourth root race, Vaivasvata Manu and his consort are the Manus for the fifth root race, and the God and Goddess Meru are the Manus for the sixth root race. The seventh root race is destined to incarnate on the continent of South America in the Aquarian age under their Manus, the Great Divine Director and his divine complement.

Manvantara. (Sanskrit, from *manv* [used in compounds for *manu*] + *antara,* 'interval, period of time.') In Hinduism, the period or age of a *Manu,* consisting of 4,320,000 solar years; one of the fourteen intervals that constitute a kalpa (Sanskrit), a period of time covering a cosmic cycle from the origination to the destruction of a world system. In Hindu cosmology, the universe is continually evolving through periodic cycles of creation and dissolution. Creation is said to occur during the outbreath of the God of Creation, Brahma; dissolution occurs during his inbreath.

Mater. (Latin, 'mother.') See *Matter; Mother.*

Matter. The feminine (negative) polarity of the Godhead, of which the masculine (positive) polarity is Spirit. Matter acts as a chalice for the kingdom of God and is the abiding place of evolving *souls* who identify with their Lord, their *Holy Christ Self.* Matter is distinguished from matter (lowercase m)—the substance of the earth earthy, of the realms of maya, which blocks rather than radiates divine light and the Spirit of the *I AM THAT I AM.* See also *Mother; Spirit.*

Mental body. One of the *four lower bodies* of man, corresponding to the air element and the second quadrant of *Matter;* the body that is intended to be the vehicle, or vessel, for the mind of God or the *Christ* Mind. "Let this [Universal] Mind be in you, which was also in Christ Jesus" (Phil. 2:5). Until quickened, this body remains the vehicle for the carnal mind, often called the lower mental body in contrast to the Higher Mental Body, a synonym for the *Christ Self* or *Christ* consciousness.

Messenger. Evangelist. One who goes before the *angels* bearing to the people of earth the good news of the gospel of Jesus Christ and, at the appointed time, the Everlasting Gospel. The Messengers of the *Great White Brotherhood* are anointed by the *Hierarchy* as their apostles ("one sent on a mission"). They deliver through the *dictations* (prophecies) of the *Ascended Masters* the testimony and lost teachings of Jesus Christ in the power of the Holy Spirit to the seed of *Christ*, the lost sheep of the house of Israel, and to every nation. A Messenger is one who is trained by an Ascended Master to receive by various methods the words, concepts, teachings and messages of the Great White Brotherhood; one who delivers the Law, the prophecies and the dispensations of God for a people and an age.

Microcosm. (Greek, 'small world.') (1) The world of the individual, his *four lower bodies,* his aura and the forcefield of his karma; or (2) The planet. See also *Macrocosm.*

Mother. "Divine Mother," "Universal Mother" and "Cosmic Virgin" are alternate terms for the feminine polarity of the Godhead, the manifestation of God as Mother. *Matter* is the feminine polarity of *Spirit,* and the term is used interchangeably with Mater (Latin, 'mother'). In this context, the entire material cosmos becomes the womb of creation into which Spirit projects the energies of life. Matter, then, is the womb of the Cosmic Virgin, who, as the other half of the Divine Whole, also exists in Spirit as the spiritual polarity of God.

Nirvana. The goal of life according to Hindu and Buddhist philosophy: the state of liberation from the wheel of rebirth through the extinction of desire.

OM (AUM). The Word; the sound symbol for ultimate Reality.

Omega. See *Alpha and Omega.*

Path. The strait gate and narrow way that leadeth unto life (Matt. 7:14). The path of initiation whereby the disciple who pursues the Christ consciousness overcomes step by step the limitations of selfhood in time and space and attains reunion with Reality through the ritual of the *ascension.*

Pearls of Wisdom. Weekly letters of instruction dictated by the *Ascended Masters* to their *Messengers* Mark L. Prophet and

Elizabeth Clare Prophet for students of the sacred mysteries throughout the world. *Pearls of Wisdom* have been published by *The Summit Lighthouse* continuously since 1958. They contain both fundamental and advanced teachings on *cosmic law* with a practical application of spiritual truths to personal and planetary problems.

Physical body. The most dense of the *four lower bodies* of man, corresponding to the earth element and the fourth quadrant of *Matter.* The physical body is the vehicle for the soul's sojourn on earth and the focus for the crystallization in form of the energies of the *etheric, mental* and *emotional bodies.*

Rays. Beams of *light* or other radiant energy. The light emanations of the Godhead that, when invoked in the name of God or in the name of the *Christ,* burst forth as a flame in the world of the individual. Rays may be projected by the God consciousness of ascended or unascended beings through the *chakras* and the third eye as a concentration of energy taking on numerous God-qualities, such as love, truth, wisdom, healing, and so on. Through the misuse of God's energy, practitioners of black magic project rays having negative qualities, such as death rays, sleep rays, hypnotic rays, disease rays, psychotronic rays, the evil eye, and so on. See also *Seven rays.*

Real Self. The *Christ Self;* the *I AM Presence;* immortal *Spirit* that is the animating principle of all manifestation. See also *Chart of Your Divine Self.*

Reembodiment. The rebirth of a *soul* in a new human body. The soul continues to return to the physical plane in a new body temple until she balances her karma, attains self-mastery, overcomes the cycles of time and space, and finally reunites with the *I AM Presence* through the ritual of the *ascension.*

Retreat. A focus of the *Great White Brotherhood,* usually on the *etheric plane* where the *Ascended Masters* preside. Retreats anchor one or more flames of the Godhead as well as the momentum of the Masters' service and attainment for the balance of *light* in the *four lower bodies* of a planet and its evolutions. Retreats serve many functions for the councils of the *Hierarchy* ministering to the lifewaves of earth. Some retreats are open to unascended mankind, whose *souls* may journey to these focuses in their *etheric body* between their incarnations on earth and in their finer bodies during sleep or *samadhi.*

Root race. See *Manu.*

Sacred fire. The Kundalini fire that lies as the coiled serpent in the base-of-the-spine *chakra* and rises through spiritual purity and self-mastery to the crown chakra, quickening the spiritual centers on the way. God, *light,* life, energy, the *I AM THAT I AM.* "Our God is a consuming fire" (Heb. 12:29). The sacred fire is the precipitation of the Holy Ghost for the baptism of souls, for purification, for alchemy and transmutation, and for the realization of the *ascension,* the sacred ritual whereby the *soul* returns to the One.

Samadhi. (Sanskrit, literally "putting together": "uniting") In Hinduism, a state of profound concentration or absorption resulting in perfect union with God; the highest state of yoga. In Buddhism, samadhis are numerous modes of concentration believed to ultimately result in higher spiritual powers and the attainment of enlightenment, or nirvana.

Sanat Kumara. (From the Sanskrit, 'always a youth.') Great *Guru* of the seed of *Christ* throughout cosmos; hierarch of Venus; the Ancient of Days spoken of in Daniel 7. Long ago he came to earth in her darkest hour when all light had gone out in her evolutions, for there was not a single individual on the planet who gave adoration to the God Presence. Sanat Kumara and the band of 144,000 souls of light who accompanied him volunteered to keep the flame of life on behalf of earth's people. This they vowed to do until the children of God would respond to the love of God and turn once again to serve their mighty *I AM Presence.* Sanat Kumara's retreat, Shamballa, was established on an island in the Gobi Sea, now the Gobi Desert. The first to respond to his flame was Gautama *Buddha,* followed by Lord Maitreya and Jesus. See also *Lord of the World.*

Seamless garment. Body of *light* beginning in the heart of the *I AM Presence* and descending around the *crystal cord* to envelop the individual in the vital currents of the *ascension* as he invokes the holy energies of the Father for the return home to God. Also known as the deathless solar body.

Secret chamber of the heart. The sanctuary of meditation behind the heart *chakra*, the place to which the *souls* of Lightbearers withdraw. It is the nucleus of life where the individual stands face to face with the inner *Guru,* the beloved *Holy Christ Self,* and receives the soul testings that precede the alchemical union with that Holy Christ Self—the marriage of the soul to the Lamb.

Seed Atom. The focus of the Divine *Mother* (the feminine ray of the Godhead) that anchors the energies of *Spirit* in *Matter* at the base-of-the-spine *chakra.* See also *Sacred fire.*

Seven rays. The *light* emanations of the Godhead; the seven *rays* of the white light that emerge through the prism of the *Christ* consciousness.

Siddhis. Spiritual powers such as levitation, stopping the heartbeat, clairvoyance, clairaudience, materialization and bilocation. The cultivation of siddhis for their own sake is often cautioned against by spiritual teachers.

Solar Logoi. *Cosmic Beings* who transmit the *light* emanations of the Godhead flowing from *Alpha and Omega* in the *Great Central Sun* to the planetary systems. Also called Solar Lords.

Soul. God is a *Spirit,* and the soul is the living potential of God. The soul's demand for free will and her separation from God resulted in the descent of this potential into the lowly estate of the flesh. Sown in dishonor, the soul is destined to be raised in honor to the fullness of that God-estate that is the one Spirit of all life. The soul can be lost; Spirit can never die.

The soul remains a fallen potential that must be imbued with the Reality of Spirit, purified through prayer and supplication, and returned to the glory from which it descended and to the unity of the Whole. This rejoining of soul to Spirit is the *alchemical marriage* that determines the destiny of the self and makes it one with immortal Truth. When this ritual is fulfilled, the highest Self is enthroned as the Lord of Life, and the potential of God, realized in man, is found to be the All-in-all.

Spirit. The masculine polarity of the Godhead; the coordinate of *Matter;* God as Father, who of necessity includes within the polarity of himself God as *Mother,* and hence is known as the *Father-Mother God.* The plane of the *I AM Presence,* of perfection; the dwelling place of the *Ascended Masters* in the kingdom of God. (When lowercased, as in "spirits," the term is synonymous with discarnates, or astral *entities;* "spirit," singular and lowercased, is used interchangeably with soul.)

Spoken Word. The *Word* of the Lord God released in the original fiats of Creation. The release of the energies of the Word, or the *Logos,* through the throat *chakra* by the Sons of God in confirmation of that lost Word. It is written, "By thy words thou shalt be justified, and by thy words thou shalt be condemned" (Matt. 12:37). Today disciples use the power of the Word in *decrees,* affirmations, prayers and *mantras* to draw the essence of the *sacred fire* from the *I AM Presence,* the *Christ Self* and *Cosmic Beings* to channel God's *light* into matrices of transmutation and transformation for constructive change in the planes of *Matter.*

The Summit Lighthouse. An outer organization of the *Great White Brotherhood* founded by Mark L. Prophet in 1958 in Washington, D.C., under the direction of the *Ascended Master* El Morya, Chief of the Darjeeling Council, for the purpose of publishing and disseminating the teachings of the Ascended Masters.

Threefold flame. The flame of the *Christ,* the spark of life that burns within the *secret chamber of the heart* (a secondary *chakra* behind the heart). The sacred trinity of power, wisdom and love that is the manifestation of the *sacred fire.* See also *Chart of Your Divine Self.*

Transfiguration. An initiation on the path of the *ascension* that takes place when the initiate has attained a certain balance and expansion of the *threefold flame.* Jesus' transfiguration is described in Matthew 17:1–8.

Tube of light. The white *light* that descends from the heart of the *I AM Presence* in answer to the call of man as a shield of protection for his four lower bodies and his soul evolution. See also *Chart of Your Divine Self.*

Twelve Hierarchies of the Sun. Twelve mandalas of *Cosmic Beings* ensouling twelve facets of God's consciousness, who hold the pattern of that frequency for the entire cosmos. They are identified by the names of the signs of the zodiac, as they focus their energies through these constellations. Also called the Twelve Solar Hierarchies. See also *Cosmic Clock.*

Twin flame. The *soul's* masculine or feminine counterpart conceived out of the same white-fire body, the fiery ovoid of the *I AM Presence.*

Unascended master. One who has overcome all limitations of Matter yet chooses to remain in time and space to focus the consciousness of God for lesser evolutions. See also *Bodhisattva.*

Universal Christ. The Mediator between the planes of *Spirit* and the planes of *Matter.* Personified as the *Christ Self,* he is the Mediator between the Spirit of God and the *soul* of man. The Universal Christ sustains the nexus of (the figure-eight flow of) consciousness through which the energies of the Father (Spirit) pass to his children for the crystallization (*Christ*-realization) of the God Flame by their soul's strivings in the cosmic womb (matrix) of the Mother (Matter).

Violet flame. Seventh-ray aspect of the Holy Spirit. The *sacred fire* that transmutes the cause, effect, record and memory of sin, or negative karma. Also called the flame of transmutation, of freedom and of forgiveness. See also *Decree; Chart of Your Divine Self.*

Word. The Word is the *Logos:* it is the power of God and the realization of that power incarnate in and as the Christ. The energies of the Word are released by devotees of the Logos in the ritual of the science of the *spoken Word.* It is through the Word that the *Father-Mother* God communicates with mankind. The Christ is the personification of the Word. See also *Christ; Decree.*

World Teacher. Office in *Hierarchy* held by those Ascended Beings whose attainment qualifies them to represent the universal and personal *Christ* to unascended mankind. The office of World Teacher, formerly held by Maitreya, was passed to Jesus and his disciple Saint Francis (Kuthumi) on January 1, 1956, when the mantle of *Lord of the World* was transferred from *Sanat Kumara* to Gautama *Buddha* and the office of *Cosmic Christ* and Planetary Buddha (formerly held by Gautama) was simultaneously filled by Lord Maitreya. Serving under Lord Maitreya, Jesus and Kuthumi are responsible in this cycle for setting forth the teachings leading to individual self-mastery and the Christ consciousness. They sponsor all *souls* seeking union with God, tutoring them in the fundamental laws governing the cause-effect sequences of their own karma and teaching them how to come to grips with the day-to-day challenges of their individual dharma, the duty to fulfill the Christ potential through the sacred labor.

The Y in the Path. The point on the path of initiation at which the individual must elect to take the right-handed path or the left-handed path.

At a certain point on the path of initiation when the individual has full awareness of the *Christ* and the full awareness of the darkness and the carnal mind, the choice is given of deciding for or against the *I AM Presence* and the Brotherhood, for or against the false hierarchy. This point is known as the Y in the path. It is the point of the initiation where one becomes *Christ* or Antichrist.

On the right-handed path one takes the knowledge of the Brotherhood, the initiations and the energies of the I AM Presence and uses these solely to the glory of the Flame and to the service of humanity. On the left-handed path the individual takes all of these things and uses them to the glory of the ego. The right-handed path is exemplified in the life of Jesus, in which all that he had was offered in service to mankind.

Climb the Highest Mountain: The Path of the Higher Self

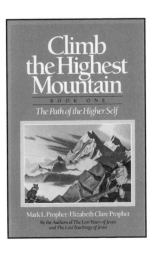

This first volume in the *Climb the Highest Mountain* series has become a classic of metaphysical literature. It explores a cornucopia of topics important to every spiritual seeker—the destiny of the soul, the difference between soul and Spirit, the role of the Christ and how to contact the Higher Self and the spark within the heart. The text is complemented by charts, tables and a comprehensive index.

ISBN: 0-916766-26-8 Paperback, 650 pages

The Path of Self-Transformation

The second volume in the series continues the authors' teachings on the inner mysteries of God. It lifts the veil and reveals the true understanding of biblical allegory, including the mystical meaning of the "fall" of Adam and Eve. It answers profound spiritual questions that are supremely relevant for today. Who suppressed the concepts of karma and reincarnation and why are they key to our spiritual growth? What is the inner meaning of the judgment? Why wasn't sex the original sin? Above all, this work is about archetypes that are key to your soul's reaching its full potential.

ISBN: 0-922729-54-9 Paperback, 358 pages

The Masters and the Spiritual Path

There are Masters who have come out of all the world's great spiritual traditions. These great lights of East and West have graduated from earth's schoolroom and reunited with Spirit in the process known as the ascension. The Masters tell us that they are examples and not exceptions to the rule. We, too, are destined to fulfill our life's purpose and reunite with Spirit. This intriguing work offers an innovative perspective on the universe and your role in it:

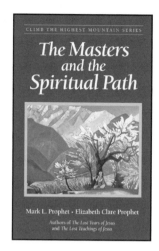

- The relationship between the ascension, nirvana and samadhi
- The parallel structure of the spiritual and material universes
- The difference between ascended and unascended masters
- The function of the spiritual hierarchy and the role of the Masters
- A unique meditation on the bliss of union with Spirit
- A breathing exercise to help you balance and expand consciousness

ISBN: 0-922729-64-6   Paperback, 360 pages

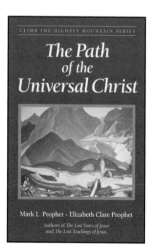

The Path of the Universal Christ

In this volume the authors of the best-selling *Lost Years of Jesus* and *Lost Teachings of Jesus* recapture the heart of the Master's message: that you, like Jesus, are meant to realize your own innate Divinity, that you are destined to become one with your own Higher Self, your "Christ Self." Church fathers suppressed Jesus' original teaching on the Christ within. But, today, Mark and Elizabeth Prophet reveal our true identity and the true goal of our life on earth.

ISBN: 0-922729-81-6   Paperback, 288 pages

Other Titles from
SUMMIT UNIVERSITY 🌙 PRESS

Fallen Angels and the Origins of Evil

Saint Germain's Prophecy for the New Millennium

The Lost Years of Jesus

The Lost Teachings of Jesus (4 vols.)

The Human Aura

Saint Germain on Alchemy

The Science of the Spoken Word

Kabbalah: Key to Your Inner Power

Reincarnation: The Missing Link in Christianity

Quietly Comes the Buddha

Lords of the Seven Rays

Prayer and Meditation

The Chela and the Path

Mysteries of the Holy Grail

POCKET GUIDES TO PRACTICAL SPIRITUALITY

Alchemy of the Heart

Your Seven Energy Centers

Soul Mates and Twin Flames

How to Work with Angels

Creative Abundance

Violet Flame to Heal Body, Mind and Soul

The Creative Power of Sound

Access the Power of Your Higher Self

For More Information

Summit University Press books are available at fine bookstores worldwide and at your favorite on-line bookseller.

If you would like a free catalog of Summit University Press books, please contact Summit University Press, PO Box 5000, Corwin Springs, MT 59030-5000 U.S.A. Telephone: 1-800-245-5445 (406-848-9500 outside the U.S.A.) Fax: 1-800-221-8307 (406-848-9555 outside the U.S.A.) Web site: www.summituniversitypress.com E-mail: info@summituniversitypress.com

Mark L. Prophet and Elizabeth Clare Prophet are pioneers of modern spirituality and internationally renowned authors. Among their best-selling titles are *The Lost Years of Jesus, The Lost Teachings of Jesus, The Human Aura, Saint Germain On Alchemy, Fallen Angels and the Origins of Evil* and the Pocket Guides to Practical Spirituality series, which includes *How to Work with Angels, Your Seven Energy Centers* and *Soul Mates and Twin Flames.* Their books are now translated into twenty languages and are available in more than thirty countries.